Contents

1 A Type—What's That? 5

2 The Numbers Game 14

3 Type of the Trinity 23

4 A Picture of Salvation 32

5 A Typical Building 41

6 Provision for Cleansing 50

7 When Divine and Human Meet 59

8 A Special Place for Special People 68

9 Into the Presence of God 77

10 Our Great Representative 86

11 The Way Through the Wilderness 94

12 The Only Way to God 102

13 Happy Holidays 110

Glossary of Types 119

Illustration: The Tabernacle Furniture 123

1
A Type—What's That?

Get ready for some good, solid steak dinners.

The Bible points out that there are basically two kinds of diet as far as truth is concerned. Hebrews 5:12-14 describes them as milk for the spiritually immature and meat (deeper teaching) for those who have matured spiritually.

Your mind will take longer to digest the truths found in typology, but they will do far more for you spiritually than the simpler truths that are the spiritual diet for most Christians.

Some years ago a congregation broke into laughter when I said it seemed about all the Bible some people know is the Book of Psalms. I learned later there was a well-known woman in the church who constantly proclaimed her love for the psalms.

Now, there's nothing wrong with the psalms. I enjoy them and have derived much inspiration and comfort from them. But the entire Bible is inspired. Why not investigate some of its deeper truths?

What Do We Mean by Typology?

Three words found in our English Bible will help us: *shadow*, *example*, and *pattern*.

Shadow. Hebrews 10:1 speaks of "the law having a

shadow of good things to come." The word *shadow* means an indistinct resemblance; a vague, dim outline.

Example. First Corinthians 10:11 states that the things that happened to the Israelites in Old Testament times were examples. The Greek word for *example* can also mean "type."

Pattern. The writer of the Book of Hebrews reminds his readers that God urged Moses to make the tabernacle and the other things necessary for worship according to the design He had shown him on Mt. Sinai. The word *pattern* means a sketch, plan, or draft. We could describe it as a blueprint or a working model.

Here's a simple definition. A *type* is a person or thing in the Bible that God designed to represent or picture some person, thing, or event that would appear in the future.

Usually, the type appears in the Old Testament and refers to something in the New Testament. I guess we can call types a sort of prophecy, giving a preview of what was coming. The many types of Jesus that appear in the Old Testament were certainly prophetic of what He would be and do.

Then there are symbols. Sometimes it's hard to tell the difference between types and symbols. In fact, the dictionary uses them as synonyms for each other. But there's a slight difference. A type is sort of a model of the thing it refers to. It has certain characteristics of the real thing. On the other hand, a symbol is an object that reminds us of something else but doesn't exactly resemble it.

Now let's look at some basic types that are found throughout the Bible.

Typical Colors

Blue-ribbon Christians. It's easy to understand why blue is considered the heavenly color. Just look up at the sky on a sunny summer day, and you'll know why.

Blue reminds us of Jesus' heavenly nature. He told the people of His day that He was the "bread of God . . .which cometh down from heaven" (John 6:33). He often spoke about heaven, beginning His famous prayer, "Our Father which art in heaven" (Matthew 6:9).

In his Gospel, John reminds us of Jesus' heavenly origin: "In the beginning was the Word, and the Word was with God, and the Word was God" (1:1). Then he goes on to say in verse 14: "And the Word was made flesh, and dwelt among us."

Jesus lived on earth for more than 33 years, but His heart was in heaven. His body was a thin veil for His deity.

The Prince and the Pauper. Mark Twain's famous book tells how the son of the king of England happened to exchange places with the son of a poor man. The bewildered pauper was treated with all the respect and honor due the heir to the throne, while the young prince wandered over the countryside trying to convince people he was the son of the king. The rags of his poverty concealed the fact of his royalty.

What a picture of what happened to Jesus, the Prince of heaven. "Though he was rich, yet for your sakes he became poor, that ye through his poverty might be rich" (2 Corinthians 8:9). But there is one major difference between our Lord and Mark Twain's hero. The fictional figure became poor through chance, but Jesus deliberately *chose* to humble himself.

We are to be heavenly people too. Not so heavenly minded that we are no earthly good, but reminding ourselves that heaven is our real home. "This world is not my home" should be more than a song.

Numbers 15:37-40 states that God commanded His people to put ribbons of blue on the hems of their garments. This was to remind them they were a special people who belonged to Him and that they were to obey His commandments.

We don't have to wear blue ribbons today, but there should be something about us that shows we are a special breed, a heavenly people.

Citizens of two countries. We all take pride in our country and feel like cheering when our flag goes by. But we are citizens of another land also. "Our conversation [citizenship] is in heaven" (Philippians 3:20). Although we owe allegiance to our native or adopted country, we owe an even higher loyalty to our heavenly country.

Our second birth is from above. Like Abraham of old, we are looking for a city far greater than any to be found in this world.

The Royal Color

Purple speaks of royalty. Judges 8:26 speaks of the "purple raiment that was on the kings of Midian." When the king of Persia honored Queen Esther's relative Mordecai, he was dressed "with a garment of fine linen and purple" (Esther 8:15). When King Belshazzar honored Daniel for interpreting the writing on the wall, he clothed him with scarlet, a color that is translated "purple" elsewhere (Daniel 5:29). To wear clothing of this color was a badge of honor.

As a type, purple speaks of the royalty of Christ. I've already mentioned how the Prince became a pauper. Because He voluntarily humbled himself, God has "highly exalted him, and given him a name which is above every name" (Philippians 2:9). When announcing to Mary that she would become the mother of the Messiah, the angel told her that God would give Jesus the throne of David and that His kingdom would know no end.

Paul joins the refrain, lauding Jesus as "the blessed and only Potentate, the King of kings, and Lord of lords" (1 Timothy 6:15). Revelation 11:15 echoes this prophecy as the angelic anthem swells: "The kingdoms of this world are become the kingdoms of our Lord, and of his Christ; and he shall reign for ever and ever."

Whenever you see purple mentioned in the Bible, let your heart thrill as you remember the coming rule of Jesus on this earth.

The Color of Suffering

Scarlet, the deep-red color of blood, was obtained in an unusual way. Along the shores of the eastern Mediterranean coast, a shellfish called the murex abounds in stupendous numbers. The Phoenicians of ancient times learned how to obtain a deep red dye by crushing multiplied thousands of these tiny sea creatures. With this background, it is easy to understand why scarlet refers to the sufferings of Christ.

The sacrifice of the Son of God did not just happen; it was divinely foreordained. Peter said that Jesus was "delivered by the determinate counsel and foreknowledge of God" (Acts 2:23).

The Old Testament constantly foreshadows the coming sacrifice of Jesus. The multiplied thousands of sheep offered on the smoking altars of Israel pointed forward to the coming of "the Lamb of God, which taketh away the sin of the world" (John 1:29).

Every time a Passover lamb was slain each year, reminding the Israelites of their deliverance from Egypt, it pointed forward to the deliverance from sin that "Christ our passover" would accomplish (1 Corinthians 5:7).

The Color of Purity

It's easy to see why white should typify purity or righteousness. It reminds us of Jesus "who did no sin, neither was guile found in his mouth" (1 Peter 2:22). Hebrews 7:26 adds that he was "holy, harmless, undefiled, separate from sinners, and made higher than the heavens." Though He was "in all points tempted like as we are," yet He was "without sin" (4:15).

But I have even better news for you than that Jesus is pure and righteous. It is that He is able to impart His righteousness to us. First Corinthians 1:30 states that among other things He is made righteousness to us.

You don't have to just admire Jesus from afar and wish you could be like Him. Okay, so you don't have any goodness of yourself. The Bible agrees with you on that score. Your own righteousness is like "filthy rags" (Isaiah 64:6). But you can receive Jesus' righteousness.

By the power of the Holy Spirit (notice the adjective *holy*), you can share in Christ's holiness. By His help you can live as Jesus would. Then what a day it will be at the Marriage Supper of the Lamb, when we celebrate our victory over the world, the flesh, and the devil.

Speaking of white, listen to this: At the wedding feast the bride of Christ (believers) will be "arrayed in fine linen, clean and white: for the fine linen is the righteousness of saints" (Revelation 19:8).

Typical Metals

As you will see later on, the tabernacle Moses erected in the wilderness is the source for much typical truth. This is especially true of the metals used in its construction.

The Gold of Divine Glory

If you ever go to Cairo, the capital of Egypt, be sure to visit the famous museum. It was built to house what are perhaps the greatest archaeological treasures in the world, mainly those found in the tomb of the pharaoh Tutankhamen. Their worth is estimated at millions of dollars.

The most fabulous of the treasures found in the tomb was the sevenfold coffin, the first coffin of solid gold. Covering the face of the royal mummy is a gold mask weighing 35 pounds, with an estimated worth of $1 million. Such was the esteem put upon gold by the ancients.

Gold became the symbol of sovereignty and power. According to Esther 4:11, the royal husband of this Jewish maiden had a golden scepter.

Gold was considered the most valuable metal in ancient times. When Daniel interpreted Nebuchadnezzar's dream, he told the king he was the head of gold on the image symbolizing Gentile dominion, because the Babylonian ruler's kingdom was the greatest (Daniel 2:38).

In the New Testament, when Paul describes the kind of spiritual lives believers can build upon the foundation of Jesus Christ, he refers to gold as representing that which will receive the highest praise. (See 1 Corinthians 3:11-15.)

So gold represents the divine glory of God. In the tabernacle, which we shall study later, gold referred to the coming Saviour. Everything in the Holy Place was of gold or covered with gold. Even though wood was used for the sides of the tabernacle, the boards were covered with gold. The gold-covered boards pictured the Incarnation—Christ's humanity covered by divine glory.

The Silver of Redemption

How can we discover what silver typifies? Let's look at what happened just after the Children of Israel left Egypt. God told Moses to number the people. He also ordered that each Israelite man should give half a shekel of silver as a ransom for his soul. This silver was then used in various ways for the construction of the tabernacle.

So silver represents redemption. Peter has a great statement about this: "Ye were not redeemed with corruptible things, as silver and gold, . . . but with the precious blood of Christ, as of a lamb without blemish and without spot" (1 Peter 1:18,19).

As you read your Bible you will often find illustrated the principle of redemption through the shedding of blood: Abel's offering; Noah's sacrifice after the Flood; the ram that took the place of Isaac, when Abraham was about to sacrifice his son; the Passover lamb in Egypt; Isaiah 53—all culminating in the redeeming death of God's Lamb.

The Brass of Judgment

Notice that the "brass" referred to in the Bible was really copper. Brass in today's world is a compound of copper and zinc, and zinc wasn't available in Biblical times.

The way brass was used helps to explain its typical significance. The brazen altar in the outer court was covered with this metal. And animals were sacrificed there for the sins of God's people; judged in their place. From brass also, Moses made a serpent (Numbers 21) that brought healing for those who looked toward it. The metal called "brass" in the Bible had a great deal of strength and endurance and the ability to stand the fire.

Brass is generally considered to be a type of judgment and justice. For example, Revelation 1 depicts Jesus walking in the midst of the candlesticks (the churches) with feet like brass, as though they burned in a furnace (v. 15). Brass pictures Jesus taking our punishment on himself, so we need not be judged for our sins.

Even Geography Is Typical

Israel (a type of God's people) shows many types from her history. Consider these:

Egypt, a place of bondage and death, is a fitting type of sin and the world. Therefore, the Passover represents the death of Christ, whereby men escape from sin. The Exodus speaks of leaving the world behind.

The wilderness journeys portray the lives of defeated Christians, and Canaan portrays Spirit-filled living. Kadesh-barnea, at the border of the Promised Land where Israel failed to enter Canaan, represents the place of decision. Many have failed at a place like this.

2
The Numbers Game

No, we're not talking about horse racing or another type of gambling. This is a sure thing. It's the numbers of the Bible.

Mankind is being reduced to a series of numbers. The giant computers of today don't know your name, but they've got your number—sometimes in more ways than one.

Your Social Security office may think of you as 459-36-5210. Your gasoline credit-card office lists you as 225-4732-1. Your special bank credit card thinks of you as 4420-340-041-404. And your state drivers license bureau may have you computerized as D015-5627-0257-6965. (By the way, all these are fictional—I don't want anyone using my numbers.)

Society is playing a big numbers game. Is it part of the devil's plan to depersonalize men? Is it paving the way for the Man of Sin who will feature the special number 666? Time will tell.

God doesn't think of men as numbers. Each individual is important to Him. But He does use numbers in a special way in His Book, the Bible. By comparing Scripture with Scripture (which is the best way to study the Word), we can learn the significance of certain numbers.

The Numerology Trap

Don't go overboard on this subject of numbers in the Bible. Some go so far as to count the number of times a letter of the alphabet is found in a certain verse. How could something like this be meaningful? People mixed up in numerology usually base their figuring on an English version, usually the King James Version. But it was the original writings written in Hebrew and Greek that were inspired, not any of the versions.

It's wise not to become too engrossed in details. The Bible contains so many wonderful truths that are evident right on the surface; why stretch a point to satisfy your curiosity?

The Number of Unity

It's easy to find the significance of the numeral *one*. Ephesians 4:4-6 establishes it very well: "There is one body, and one Spirit, even as ye are called in one hope of your calling; one Lord, one faith, one baptism, one God and Father of all, who is above all, and through all, and in you all."

The gospel contains certain features on which believers can and should unite. Someone has said: "In essentials unity; in nonessentials liberty; in all things charity." That's fine, but let's make sure we keep all the essential doctrines under that banner. A river has to have banks or it becomes a flood. Unless we agree on essential doctrines, there can be chaos.

Jesus told us the importance of unity when He prayed to the Father in the Upper Room: "That they all may be one; as thou, Father, art in me, and I in thee, that they also may be one in us: that the world may believe that thou hast sent me" (John 17:21).

Jesus wasn't talking about the unity brought by an organization. There is a true Church, the Church

Universal, that crosses all organizational lines. It's composed of all true believers in Christ who have been born again by the power of the Spirit.

The Number of Completeness

Three is the number of the Trinity. Look at how this number is used in the Bible:

The Bible gives three definitions of God. He is a spirit. He is light. He is love.

The tabernacle Moses built in the wilderness was divided into three parts: the outer court, the Holy Place, and the Holy of Holies (sometimes called the Most Holy Place).

Three metals were used in the construction of the tabernacle: gold, silver, and brass.

The Bible often mentions three colors together in a special way: blue, purple, and scarlet.

The number *three* was prominent at the crucifixion of Christ. He was crucified at the third hour of the day; His accusation was written over His head in three languages; and He spent 3 days in the grave.

At God's command, the Jews celebrated three great feasts: Passover, Pentecost, and Tabernacles.

The Gospels record three instances when the Father spoke from heaven: Matthew 3:17; 17:5; John 12:28.

Jesus raised three people from the dead: Jairus' daughter, the son of the widow of Nain, and his friend Lazarus.

The Jordan River was crossed by a miracle three times: when Israel marched into Canaan; when Elijah passed over it just before his translation; and when Elisha returned after Elijah's translation.

The Number of Human Achievement

Bible scholars generally think of the numeral *six* as representing man at his highest and best.

God created man on the 6th day.

Nebuchadnezzar, as the head of gold in the dream Daniel interpreted, represents man at his zenith. And the image the King of Babylon erected, as described in Daniel 3, was 60 cubits high and 6 cubits wide.

And make no mistake about the Antichrist. He will be superb, as men reckon greatness—charismatic, intelligent, and forceful. And his number is a triple six—666 (Revelation 13:18).

The Number of Divine Perfection

Certain numbers seem to have tremendous significance in Scripture. One of these is the number *seven*. Notice these places where it occurs.

Seven men lived more than 900 years: Adam (930), Seth (912), Enos (905), Cainan (910), Jared (962), Methuselah (969), and Noah (950). (The first six are listed in Genesis 5; Noah's age at death is given in Gensis 9:29.)

God created the universe in 6 days, and on the 7th day He rested, as He "saw every thing that he had made, and, behold, it was very good" (Genesis 1:31). Later, He made the 7th day a special sign between Him and His people Israel.

God has instituted a week of 7 days as an important part of man's life cycle. The leaders of the French Revolution tried to establish a 10-day week to achieve greater production, but they had to go back to the 7-day week, with 1 day for rest. The human body was designed for a 7-day week.

The Book of Revelation almost inundates us with its "sevens." It is fitting to have so many instances here, for it is with this book that God completes His great plan of Redemption.

In Revelation you find Christ walking in the midst of the seven golden candlesticks, carrying seven stars in His right hand. There are seven letters to the churches of Asia. There are seven spirits before the throne of God. The book is sealed with seven seals. There are seven angels standing before the Throne. There are seven trumpets, seven vials, and seven thunders that utter their voices.

The Book of Revelation speaks of seven "blesseds" (1:3; 14:13; 16:15; 19:9; 20:6; 22:7,14). A reason is provided for each of these except the central one, Revelation 19:9, which says: "Blessed are they which are called unto the marriage supper of the Lamb." It seems no reason is given, or needed, since it is obvious that those called to this event are indeed greatly blessed.

The Number of Resurrection

Eight is the number of a new beginning, for after 7 days, the 8th day begins a new week. Thus, Jesus arose on the 8th day, the 1st day of the week.

An Old Testament example of this is: Noah was the eighth person from Adam, and eight persons were saved from the Flood in the ark. In a sense, it was a resurrection, a new start after the waters of the Flood had subsided.

In addition to the resurrection of Jesus, the Bible records eight other cases when people were brought back from the dead. Three are found in the Old Testament: the son of the widow of Zarephath, by Elijah (1 Kings 17:17-22); the Shunammite woman's son, by Elisha (2 Kings 4:32-37); and the man who was revived when his dead body touched the bones of Elisha (2 Kings 13:20,21).

The Gospels contain three instances of resurrection (mentioned earlier—Jairus' daughter, the son of the widow of Nain, and Lazarus). The Book of Acts tells of two others: Dorcas (9:36-41) and Eutychus (20:9-12). All these total eight.

The Number of Perfect Order

The way the number *10* is used throughout the Bible indicates it refers to systematic order and the perfection of that order.

Genesis 1 reveals the perfect order in Creation, for the phrase "and God said" occurs 10 times.

God gave the Ten Commandments to His people. If a person will keep them, they will bring a perfect order to his life.

By commanding that the Holy of Holies be a perfect cube—10 cubits wide, long, and high—God indicated He wants a perfect order in worship.

By sending 10 plagues on Egypt, God showed the perfection of order in His judgment on Pharaoh because of the ruler's hardness of heart.

The Millennium, 1,000 years, or the numeral 10 raised to the third power—10 times 10, times 10—will reveal Christ's perfect order in government.

The Number of Governmental Perfection

Twelve is the number of government. For example: Jacob had 12 sons, and though there were 13 tribes, because Joseph's two sons became tribes, the Bible never mentions more than 12 at one time.

The 12 apostles of Christ became leaders in His kingdom, the Church. He told them that if they were faithful, they would "sit on thrones judging the twelve tribes of Israel" (Luke 22:30).

When God pulls back the curtain of the future in the Book of Revelation, in chapters 4 and 5 we see 24 elders; that is, 12 doubled. They are sitting on thrones and seem to represent the saints who will rule with Christ. That is our destiny; we need to get in training by ruling ourselves now.

The number *12* reaches the apex of its meaning in the description of the New Jerusalem, which will be the seat of government for Christ's kingdom. There are 12 gates and 12 angels, and the city rests on 12 foundations. Don't stop there. The length, breadth, and height are each 12 furlongs, and the wall is 144 cubits (12 times 12). All this teaches us that God's city will have a perfect government.

The Number of Testing

One more number—*40*. Moses' life consisted of three periods of 40 years each. Israel was tested in the wilderness for 40 years. Jesus' period of temptation in the wilderness was 40 days. If we endure temptation, we shall conquer as He did.

Fireworks

Though the main emphasis of this chapter is numbers, let's think about another important symbol, *fire.*

God's presence. When God renewed His covenant with Abraham, He revealed himself in the form of a smoking furnace and a burning lamp (Genesis 15:17). It was also in fire that He revealed himself to Moses at the burning bush (Exodus 3:2) and to Israel at Sinai (19:18; 20:18-20). In each case it produced reverence. The consuming nature of fire teaches us we cannot trifle with God.

Guidance. God went before Israel in a pillar of fire by night to guide them (Numbers 9:15).

God's approval. Fire has often shown that God approved the actions of His people. Fire consumed the sacrifice at the dedication of Solomon's Temple (2 Chronicles 7:1). When Elijah on Mt. Carmel offered a burnt offering, which symbolized consecration, God showed His approval by fire (1 Kings 18:38).

On the Day of Pentecost, the fire of God appeared in the Upper Room (Acts 2:3). This indicates that when we prepare our hearts before God, He will answer.

God's judgment. God on occasion has sent fire to judge the sins of men. Sodom and Gomorrah were destroyed by fire because of their immorality (Genesis 19). His fire consumed the 250 followers of Korah, Dathan, and Abiram because they rebelled against God-given leadership (Numbers 16:35). Fire from the presence of God destroyed Aaron's sons, Nadab and Abihu, for their irreverence and presumption (Leviticus 10:1,2). And God's final judgment will be the lake of fire (Revelation 20:10,15).

Leprosy—Type of Sin

Leprosy is one of the most vivid types of sin in all the Bible, even in its details. Notice these parallels: (1) It was very prevalent. (2) Though it began small, it spread rapidly, destroying as it went. (3) It brought uncleanness and finally death. (4) Healing came by a miracle. (5) After his cleansing, the leper could come back to perfect fellowship by only one way, the way God had ordered.

Do you see the parallel with sin? The Bible tells us that all of us have sinned. Sin begins small but spreads greatly, defiling the soul. Eventually, sin leads to eternal death. There is only one way to be perfectly restored, the way of the Cross, and it takes a miracle.

A Sprinkling of Types

Oil. Throughout the Bible oil is a type of the Holy Spirit. Three types of leaders were anointed with oil, perhaps giving us a clue to God's purpose in the baptism in the Holy Spirit: (1) kings—to be leaders; (2) priests—to be mediators between God and man (for us, this would signify prayer); and (3) prophets—to be speakers for God (witnesses?). Oil was also used in the offerings and for light in the tabernacle.

Leaven. This substance is a picture of decay and spiritual corruption. In 1 Corinthians 5:8, Paul describes it as "malice and wickedness."

Salt. This is the opposite of leaven, for it was used to preserve. It also symbolizes friendship and faithfulness. God's covenant is called a "covenant of salt" (Numbers 18:19). We need to remind ourselves that we are to be "the salt of the earth." Godly people have a preserving quality. What depths society would go to if it were not for the presence of the godly!

3
Type of the Trinity

When you hear the name Abraham Lincoln, what quality does it make you think of? Integrity, for he was known as "Honest Abe."

When you hear that a boss is a "Simon Legree," what does it say to you? Probably that he is a hard taskmaster like the character in *Uncle Tom's Cabin*.

When someone speaks of Johnnie Appleseed, what do you think of? Probably of generosity, for he showed his love for others by planting a multitude of trees throughout the Midwest.

Even more than these men, certain Biblical personalities provide a meaning beyond their own lifetimes. To consider all the people who typified Biblical truth would take a large book, so we'll confine ourselves to just three. Christ is usually the central figure of the types, but the other Persons in the Trinity often figure prominently.

A Picture of Calvary

A proof of love. It's a very poignant scene that takes place at Hebron. By a miracle, for the parents were too old for childbearing, Isaac had been born to Abraham and Sarah. They had named him Isaac—"Laughter"—as God had told them, and he was the joy of their lives.

Then came a dark, dark day, for God asked Abraham to sacrifice his son on one of the mountains of Moriah, about 60 miles north, believed to be the site of present-day Jerusalem. Genesis 22 tells the story.

God left no doubt as to what He meant. Notice how precisely He impressed on the heart of the father what the sacrifice would mean to him. First He said, "Take now thy son" (v. 2). Then He added, "Thine only son." God continued, "Isaac" (there was no way out; He didn't mean Ishmael). Then He added the final blow, "Whom thou lovest." He wanted Abraham to know the cost.

Do you see the parallel? Here is a picture of God the Father giving Jesus, the only begotten Son. No one else would do—not even the highest of the angels. There was only one way to save the world—by giving the One nearest and dearest to Him, the One who brought joy and pleasure to the heavenly land.

A sacrifice on a mountain. God told Abraham the place of the offering—"the land of Moriah . . . upon one of the mountains" (v. 2).

Jerusalem is built on Mount Moriah, and the northernmost and highest point is Gordon's Calvary, one of the two possible sites for the Crucifixion.

Carrying the wood. Rather ironic, isn't it, that the proposed victim, Isaac, was asked to carry the wood on which he would be laid (v. 6)? But it reminds us of another scene. John tells us about it: "And he bearing his cross went forth into a place called the place of a skull, which is called in the Hebrew Golgotha" (19:17).

The father suffered too. Try to imagine how Abraham felt as he and Isaac climbed the lonely trail to the top of Moriah. Can you imagine how it struck home to his heart when Isaac asked: "Where is the lamb for a burnt offering?" (Genesis 22:7).

Isaac's father knew what lay ahead. *He* knew who the "lamb" was. *He* knew who must take the knife and drive it into the heart of his son. Don't you think Abraham would rather have died himself? I do.

What about God the Father at Calvary? Don't you think He grieved with His Son in Gethsemane? Don't you think He suffered too as He watched the terrible scene at Calvary?

Pilate, the high priests, and the Roman soldiers were the knife God used, but Jesus' death was the Father's responsibility. Because of His infinite capacity for loving, His suffering is infinite in its scope.

Yielding without a struggle. I wonder when Isaac finally realized he himself was to be the sacrifice. What thoughts must have raced through his mind! Did he want to escape?

One of the most amazing parts of the entire story is the submission of Isaac to his father. Abraham was an old man, past 100 years. Isaac was young and strong. Yet there is not the slightest indication that Isaac struggled, argued, or even begged, as Abraham bound him and laid him on the altar. Isaac's trust matched Abraham's faith.

Again there is the beautiful parallel at Calvary. Jesus didn't have to submit. By beckoning with one finger, even after His hands were nailed to the cross, Jesus could have brought legions of angels swooping to His rescue. It was not the nails that held Jesus on the cross. It was love. For God. For you.

The big difference. At one point the type is imperfect. Just as the knife in Abraham's hand started down, God intervened. But nothing interrupted the sacrifice of the Son of God.

Winning a Bride

Everyone enjoys a love story—and Redemption is the greatest love story ever told. All the ingredients of a drama are there: the hero, the villain, the bride. The villain almost wins, but the hero wins the victory—and the bride. And they live happily ever after.

Genesis 24, with its story of how Rebekah became the bride of Isaac, beautifully portrays how Christ is winning His bride, the Church. Actually, the servant Eliezer, who pictures the work of the Holy Spirit, is the central figure of the narrative.

A concerned father. Abraham was worried. He was getting on in years and his son Isaac didn't yet have a wife. Observing the young women of Canaan, he knew none of them would be a fitting companion for his son. Isaac was not only the heir to his father's vast possessions, he was also the heir to the promises of God. He had a special destiny, so his wife must be special.

The Scriptures describe the Church, composed of all born-again believers in Christ, as His bride. He wants her to be "a glorious church, not having spot, or wrinkle, or any such thing; but that it should be holy and without blemish" (Ephesians 5:27). The Lord is not looking for outward beauty so much, however, as inward loveliness. Our destiny is interwoven with our Lord's. We must qualify for it.

A devoted servant. How self-effacing Eliezer is in this story. He stays in the background. He thinks only of doing the will of Abraham. Notice how he pictures the work of the Holy Spirit, whose main mission in the world is to provide a Bride for the Son of God:

1. Like Eliezer, the Holy Spirit does not speak of himself (John 16:13).

2. Eliezer went on a long journey to find a bride for Isaac. The Holy Spirit is at work in all parts of the world, trying to bring people to Jesus.

3. Of Eliezer, Genesis 24:10 states: "All the goods of his master were in his hand." And at a suitable time he

lavished them on Rebekah, the prospective bride. Through the ministry of the Holy Spirit the gifts and blessings of God are given to believers.

4. Eliezer brought Rebekah to a place of decision, then she had to make the choice herself. No one could make it for her. It is by the drawing power of the Holy Spirit that people are brought to the decision whether or not to follow Christ. And the decision is theirs alone. No one can make it for them.

5. Genesis 24:61 points out that as the caravan left Haran, Rebekah followed him. It reminds us of Romans 8:14: "As many as are led by the Spirit of God, they are the sons of God."

Rebekah must have learned about Isaac from Eliezer. As he told her about her bridegroom and the place he had prepared for her, how anxious she must have become. No wonder as she saw someone coming to meet the caravan, and the servant said, "It is my master," she got off her camel and hurried to meet him. Did she consider the camel too slow?

As you and I commune with the Holy Spirit, He will fulfill Jesus' words: "He shall glorify me: for he shall receive of mine, and shall show it unto you" (John 16:14). And it will make us anxious to meet our Bridegroom.

A choice bride. Isn't it beautiful how the type matches the fulfillment? Those who qualify for the bride of Christ must meet the same requirements Eliezer looked for in Rebekah. Of primary importance, she must not be a Canaanite, she must belong to the family of Abraham. Aren't you glad you can sing, "I'm so glad I belong to the family of God"? Now, notice the other specifications:

1. Rebekah had to make the decision herself to become the bride of Isaac. No one forced her. It

amounted to having faith in what the servant said about his master and what he could offer her.

How does the Holy Spirit speak to us today? Mainly by the Word of God. It is faith in what the Bible says that gives us the impetus to leave the old life and start out for a better land.

We have to make our own decision to follow Christ. It's an act of the will as well as an act of faith. "Whom having not seen, ye love" (1 Peter 1:8).

2. Rebekah had to make the consecration to leave her home. It was an unknown path. It involved some hardships—and perhaps danger.

We are not worthy of Jesus, He said, unless we are willing to leave everything behind and put ourselves completely in His hands. And He won't fail us!

3. Finally, there came the climax of the journey as Rebekah saw Isaac in the distance, and they met, and she became his wife.

The father of Matthew Henry, the great Bible commentator, was a devout Christian. It is reported that often at the close of the day as he considered the goodness of God, he would say, "All this—and heaven too."

You think Christianity is great now? To put it in the vernacular, "You ain't seen nothin' yet." The time is coming when we who now walk by faith will see our Lord face to face, and we shall "ever be with the Lord" (1 Thessalonians 4:17).

Like the old stories always end (almost always anyway), we shall live "happily ever after."

A Parallel Person

Let's admit this first—nowhere in the Bible, as far as I can tell, is it stated that Joseph, son of Jacob, is a type of Jesus. Yet probably no other person in the Scriptures has in his life more parallels to the life and ministry of the Lord.

Doesn't it seem significant that more than one fourth of the Book of Genesis is devoted to the story of Joseph's life? Notice the similarities:

1. He was a shepherd (Genesis 37:2), and of course Jesus is the Good Shepherd.

2. His father loved him exceedingly and gave him the best he could afford (v. 3).

3. His own brothers hated him and rejected his leadership (vv. 4,8). Notice John 1:11: "He came unto his own, and his own received him not."

4. He had a "joy that was set before him" of future glorification (Hebrews 12:2; Genesis 37:7,9).

5. His father took notice of God's plans for his son, as Mary did concerning Jesus (Genesis 37:11; Luke 2:51).

6. His father sent him to his brothers (Genesis 37:13).

7. Joseph was willing to do his father's will, and so was Jesus (v. 13; Hebrews 10:7).

8. Both Joseph and Jesus went to seek their brethren (Genesis 37:16; Luke 19:10).

9. Joseph's brothers plotted against him (Genesis 37:18), as Judas plotted against Jesus.

10. As in the case of Pilate and Jesus, a leader, Reuben, though weak in character, tried to find a way to deliver Joseph.

11. Joseph was stripped of his beautiful robe (Genesis 37:23), reminding us of how the Son of God laid aside His divine prerogatives (Philippians 2:6-8).

12. Joseph was cast into a pit (Genesis 37:24), reminding us of Jesus' humiliation and His willingness to take on himself the form of a slave (Philippians 2:7).

13. Joseph's brothers "sat down to eat bread" (Genesis 37:25), reminding us of the callousness demonstrated at the cross (Matthew 27:36).

14. Joseph's brothers used foreigners to carry out their wicked plans (Genesis 37:25,28), reminding us that it was the Romans who carried out the wishes of the Jewish leaders.

15. The root of the name *Judah*, who suggested selling Joseph, is the same as the name *Judas*.

16. Joseph was sold for 20 pieces of silver (Genesis 37:28), reminding us of the silver paid to Judas.

17. Joseph became a servant (Genesis 37:36), reminding us that Jesus came to minister (Mark 10:45).

18. Joseph resisted temptation in Potiphar's house (Genesis 39:7-12), as Jesus resisted temptation in the wilderness (Matthew 4:1-10).

19. Like Jesus, Joseph suffered though innocent (Genesis 39:13-20).

20. Joseph was with two sinners in his humiliation (40:1-3).

21. Joseph became noted for his wisdom (41:39), and so was Jesus (Matthew 22:15-46).

22. Joseph saved the world from death by providing them with bread (Genesis 41:53-57); Jesus is the Bread of Life, who brings eternal life (John 6:32-36).

23. There came a time when everyone had to recognize Joseph's authority (Genesis 41:43), reminding us of the time when every knee shall bow at the mention of the name of Jesus (Philippians 2:10).

24. Eventually, Joseph's brothers had to recognize his authority (Genesis 42:6). The same will be true of Jesus.

25. Joseph's brothers had access to the king because of him (47:1,2). Jesus is our mighty Mediator (Hebrews 4:14-16).

26. Joseph's brothers were blessed for his sake (Genesis 47:5,6). Everything we receive is because of Jesus (Romans 8:32).

27. Joseph had a Gentile bride (Genesis 41:50), and it is because of Jesus that Gentiles are included in God's plan of redemption (Ephesians 2:11-19).

28. Joseph showed remarkable magnanimity when he forgave those who had done him wrong (Genesis 50:14-21), foreshadowing Jesus' statement on the cross: "Father, forgive them; for they know not what they do" (Luke 23:34).

What a delightful parallel Joseph presents of Jesus' earthly ministry.

4

A Picture of Salvation

"Noah's ark! The Flood! Who cares about that! That happened many thousands of years ago—why should it affect us?"

Would Jesus' comments on the subject mean anything to you? I hope so, for after all, He's the Son of God. What He says is important.

Listen. Jesus is speaking: "As the days of Noah were, so shall also the coming of the Son of man be" (Matthew 24:37).

Do you see what that means?

If we can notice any similarity between the conditions at the time of Flood and the kind of a world we're living in, then it certainly seems we're "headed for the last roundup." World history is headed for a smashing climax.

That's significant in itself, but the events of the Flood have another important meaning for us. Although the Bible doesn't say Noah's ark is a type, there are so many circumstances related to the ark and how Noah and his family were rescued, we're on rather safe ground in seeing it as a picture of salvation.

Dreadful Days

Those are pretty rough words the Bible uses to describe the days of Noah: "The wickedness of man was great in the earth . . . every imagination of the thoughts of his heart was only evil continually" (Genesis 6:5).

"Only evil continually." Can't get any worse than that, can you? Let's see how they got that way.

The line of Cain. After he had murdered his brother Abel, Cain left his parents' home and started a separate civilization.

Cain made a big mistake. He left God out of the picture. I'm not saying all of Cain's descendants were notorious sinners, but they all ignored God. Their civilization was completely secular, humanistic.

You know, a person can believe in God but still be a practical atheist—that is, living as though God doesn't exist. Which is about the same as actually not believing He exists.

Cain's godless line reached its climax with Lamech, the seventh generation from Adam. Utterly ignoring God, Lamech became the first polygamist, the first one to defy God's commandment by defiling the divine institution of marriage.

A welcome contrast. With a sigh of relief we turn from Cain's descendants to consider Seth and his line. They didn't deny or defy God; instead, they turned to prayer, calling on God (Genesis 4:26).

What a contrast between the seventh generation of Seth's line, as compared with Lamech's generation, the seventh in Cain's line. Seth's line reached a climax of righteousness and holiness in Enoch, who walked so close to God that one day God just took him (5:24). As someone has described it: "He said to God, I'm closer to your home than I am to mine, why don't I just go home with you to stay?"

But then the line of separation became blurred. There was intermarriage between the two lines, and instead of the Sethites being able to lift the descendants to their level, the Cainites dragged them down to their level. It always works that way, doesn't it?

Wickedness became terribly widespread. Jesus describes the conditions in part by the phrase "eating and drinking, marrying and giving in marriage" (Matthew 24:38). Some scholars say the second part of that expression means "exchanging in marriage." Again, the foundations of society were being destroyed.

Superlative wickedness. These men of Noah's time were all evil. Their sin wasn't alleviated by anything good. There were no parenthetical periods of goodness or righteousness.

Those dreadful days were also characterized by terrible deeds. "The earth was filled with violence" (Genesis 6:11). Those who break the laws of God are not likely to keep the laws of man. Brute force seems to have been on the throne. Human life meant nothing. It was a time of cruel bloodletting.

What was the cause of all this? Scripture tells us in the phrase "all flesh had corrupted his way upon the earth" (v. 12).

Sin is often a corruption of things not necessarily wrong in themselves. Love is not wrong, but corrupted it becomes lust. Desire is not wrong, but corrupted it becomes covetousness. Ambition to excel is not wrong in itself, but corrupted it leads to jealousy, strife, variance, and hatred.

In Noah's time, men had taken all that God had given them—pure, clean, good things—and had perverted them by their corrupt desires.

The conditions of Noah's day are a picture of what is happening in today's world. The sewer of sin is overflowing and flooding the streets of our cities and towns.

Crime is running rampant. Sex crimes are increasing, and alcoholism continues its upward climb. Men flout the law of the land. Authorities wink at immorality.

Wasn't Jesus a good prophet?

You Can't Sin and Get By

Men had gone too far. God could not let them go any farther. They were about to annihilate themselves anyway. It was time for judgment.

This was a tremendous catastrophe, worldwide in its scope. The histories of nearly every nation contain an account of such a deluge: the Mexicans, Eskimos, Chinese, the people of Malaysia, the Chaldeans, and the Egyptians. In the Creation period, water had once covered the earth, and God had caused the dry land to appear (Genesis 1:9). But now the earth was going to sink back beneath the waters.

God was going to do a laundry job on the earth. It was going to have a fresh beginning.

The Flood was universal. If some question this, it is enough to note that God spoke of it as destroying "all flesh, wherein is the breath of life, from under heaven" (6:17). Not one creature would escape except those safe within the ark.

"The wages of sin is death" (Romans 6:23), and one thing you can say about the devil, he won't shortchange those who work for him. They'll get paid in full measure. The Flood meant doom to every person outside the ark, and every person outside of Christ will also suffer death—eternal death.

But God is merciful. How long does a person need to get ready for death? God gave Noah's generation 120 years—and it still wasn't long enough for some.

This is the way God works. Though He is just and will

judge those with sin, He always gives people a chance to hear and believe.

There's a Way of Escape

It's pretty easy to see in the ark a parallel to the salvation Christ brings to us.

There was room for all. Rather close quarters, I guess, when all the animals got in the ark, but it was still adequate for all who came.

God isn't some monster waiting to clobber everyone who does wrong. He's the very essence of love, "long-suffering to us-ward, not willing that any should perish, but that all should come to repentance" (2 Peter 3:9).

Whenever God has sent judgment, He has always made a provision for His people and for those who wanted to repent. He did it at Sodom. And He did it for Rahab and her family at Jericho. "There's Room at the Cross for You" is more than a great song, it's a wonderful fact.

God's a good Architect. The One who designed the countless stars and constellations of the heavens had no difficulty designing a small ark. He planned it exactly, giving Noah the specific dimensions.

God even planned to have only one door in the ark (Genesis 6:16). There was only one way to get in. It reminds us, doesn't it, of the many passages of Scripture that teach the same truth: "I am *the* way" (John 14:6). "Neither is there salvation in any other: for there is *none* other name under heaven given among men, whereby we must be saved" (Acts 4:12).

God has planned salvation very exactly. There's no need to try to improvise on God's plan. There's no other way except through the blood sacrifice of Jesus.

Fear's Not All Bad

"Don't try to scare people into heaven," people sometimes advise. But maybe we ought to scare people a little more.

Don't you think a Christless eternity is something to bring fear? Don't you think hell is something that *should* scare a sinner?

Noah didn't consider himself above fear. "Noah, . . . moved with fear, prepared an ark to the saving of his house" (Hebrews 11:7).

I imagine Mrs. Noah and Shem, Ham, and Japheth, and their wives were mighty glad Noah got scared about the coming judgment.

Fear may not be the highest motive, but it's a worthy one—and effective.

Obedience Pays Off

It wasn't any easy job building an ark in those days. Can you imagine the kind of tools they used? Even with power tools it would be hard to build a vessel that large in these days. Imagine how they labored to complete the ship.

Think of what toil it must have been for them to cut down tree after tree to form the framework of the ark—and using crude tools. Then they had to trim the logs to make them smooth, and then cut them to size.

Noah obeyed, even though the ark may have seemed to be too large a vessel. He built it exactly as the divine Architect had stated. He gathered the animals as God had commanded and took his family inside the ark.

No one can be saved without obeying God. Those who receive the promises of salvation must also obey its commands.

God can't welcome those who won't come.

He can't forgive those who won't repent.

He can't cleanse those who won't confess their sins.

He can't bring into His family those who won't give up the world.

It's as simple as that.

Faith That Doesn't Question

Why did Noah obey God? It's simple—because he *believed* Him. It was "by faith" he prepared an ark. And look at how much more we have on which to base our faith. Noah had only the spoken word of God. We have the written Word of God, the Bible. If we believe the written Word as Noah obeyed the spoken word, we too will obey.

Noah had to deal with many obstacles to his faith. After all, it did look rather silly to build a boat like this so far from the water. Noah's associates might well have argued with him, "Do you think God would destroy the world such a short time after creating it?"

Noah may have had to struggle with his views on the mercy of God. Would the God he knew really destroy all mankind from the earth? And what was this about a flood so great it would cover the whole earth? (Some scholars believe it had not rained up to this time.)

And there was the ridicule—one of the devil's most effective weapons. Certainly Noah's contemporaries had plenty to laugh about.

When Fulton first invented the steamboat men ridiculed the invention, calling it "Fulton's Folly." But time proved Fulton correct. The men of Noah's day might well have called the ark "Noah's Notion." But as in the case of Fulton, time vindicated Noah. When the rain began to pelt down, the scoffers began to wish they had heeded Noah's advice—but it was too late.

Ridicule and scorn must never discourage us from following the path God has chosen for us.

The way God has designed for men to be saved seems foolish to those who harden their hearts against their Creator. It seems to be against reason. "How can the death of one man 2,000 years ago help someone like me today?" a person might ask. Paul was correct: "The preaching of the cross is to them that perish, foolishness" (1 Corinthians 1:18). Yet when men come to the Cross as the means of salvation, they find God's way will work for them.

When God Shuts the Door

Finally, the miracle of gathering all the animals and fowl had been completed. Noah and his family were safe inside the ark. Then came the awesome time when God himself shut the door (Genesis 7:16). The divine Doorkeeper swung shut the door of mercy.

The clouds became darker. The rain began to fall—gently at first, but increasing in intensity until it was a downpour, then a cloudburst, and at last a deluge.

It didn't take long for the scoffers to change their minds. They pounded on the door of the ark, frantically trying to get inside. But it was too late. As in the case of the foolish virgins of Matthew 25, once the door was shut there was no second chance.

The Great Invitation

Come is one of the great words of the Bible. It has been made into an acrostic:

    C stands for Children
    O stands for Old People
    M stands for Middle-aged People
    E stands for Everybody

No one is excluded. It was God himself who said to Noah: "*Come* thou and all thy house into the ark" (Genesis 7:1). Over and over throughout the pages of the grand old Book, the word *come* rings out, until in the very last chapter of Revelation we read: "And the Spirit and the bride say, Come. And let him that heareth say, Come. And let him that is athirst come. And whosoever will, let him take the water of life freely" (22:17).

Judgment fell, and though the earth was destroyed, the ark sailed serenely along. The ark was covered with pitch to keep the water out. The word *pitch* comes from a Hebrew word meaning "to cover" and is translated "atonement" in other parts of the Old Testament. As the pitch protected the ark from the waters of judgment, the blood of Christ's atonement saves us from the condemnation we deserve because of our sins.

5
A Typical Building

You won't find a better source for studying types than the tabernacle Moses erected following God's blueprint. Every part of the structure is a type, and every item it contained. Everywhere we look we see a picture of something contained in the gospel, and especially the Lord Jesus Christ.

Let's not hurry. Let's walk leisurely through this building and enjoy the treasure of types that leap into view. Think of it as the biggest visual-aid board in history.

A Special Building

And it was *that*. God's people had been in Egypt for centuries, and they needed to learn about His plans for them. The tabernacle spelled out in simple language the purpose and message of God—redemption for all mankind. Through the tabernacle, God taught Israel the ABC's of His plan of Redemption.

You don't think the tabernacle is important? God did—enough to use 15 chapters of the Bible to describe its details.

"Why did God need a building anyway? After all, He fills the entire universe."

You're right! God didn't need a building. But *man* did. The tabernacle was a place where God could localize himself for the benefit of His people. Here would be the place where His presence in the form of the Shekinah would dwell. Here was a place where people could meet with God.

By its very structure the tabernacle taught the Israelites something about God. There was a special room in this special building that belonged only to God, and from which they were excluded. By this they were impressed with the holiness of God and their own sinfulness.

Yet they also learned that there was a way by which they could approach God—the way of sacrifice. A good lesson for us. there's only one way to draw near to God, through the great Sacrifice—Christ and His shed blood (Hebrews 10:19-22).

The Names Are Important

The very names the Scriptures use for the tabernacle show its purpose:

1. *The sanctuary* (Exodus 25:8). This showed it was a holy place.

2. *The tabernacle* (v. 9). This meant it was a dwelling place for God, a place where God would live. You can find the same thought in John 1:14: "The Word was made flesh, and dwelt [tabernacled] among us."

3. *The tent* (Exodus 40:2). It was a temporary arrangement. Later, the temple would take its place, and eventually the gospel, which it pictured, would supersede it. Actually, *all* the Old Testament provisions were temporary, serving a useful purpose until the perfect arrangement came.

4. *The tent of testimony* (Numbers 9:15). This was because the Ten Commandments had been placed in the ark of the covenant, and it was located in the Holy of

Holies. The two tablets of stone were called the "testimony" (Exodus 31:18; 34:29). The entire purpose of the tabernacle was to testify concerning God's holiness, man's sinfulness, and God's plan of atonement through sacrifice. And isn't that the gospel?

5. *House of God* (Judges 18:31). This was during the days when the judges ruled Israel. The nation of Israel was no longer in the wilderness; they were in Canaan. God had established His residence there.

It Didn't Come Cheap

Don't let the fact that the tabernacle was sort of a tent fool you as to its cost. It's true, we don't know just how much gold, silver, and brass was worth in those ancient times, and we can't figure the value of the wood, fabrics, precious stones, skins, oil, and dyes. So, we can't put an exact value on the tabernacle. But it was a beautiful place. Estimates of its cost range from $1 to $1½ million. Some go as high as $2 million. And remember the low economic values of those days. The tabernacle must have been luxurious and lovely, the very best place that could be provided as the residence of God.

Three's Are Everywhere

As I said in chapter 2, three is the number of Deity, of the Trinity. Wherever we go in the tabernacle we'll find the numeral *three* predominant. Since the tabernacle is a picture story of God's plan of Redemption, the prevalence of three emphasizes the interest and the work of the Trinity in the plan of salvation.

1. There were three sections to the tabernacle: the outer court, the Holy Place, and the Most Holy Place (also called the Holy of Holies).

2. There were three doors: one into the outer court, where the altar was; one into the Holy Place, where the priests served; and one into the Holy of Holies, which typified God's presence.

3. There were three kinds of light: the light of the sun in the outer court; the light of the golden candlestick in the Holy Place; and the light of the Shekinah in the Holy of Holies.

4. The blood was sprinkled in three different places: on the brazen altar, on the golden altar of incense, and on the mercy seat.

5. Three basic metals were used in the tabernacle: gold, speaking of divinity; silver, speaking of Redemption; and brass, speaking of judgment.

6. Three basic colors were used: scarlet, typifying atonement; blue, typifying heaven; and purple, typifying royalty. In addition, white (which is not really a color) was prominent, typifying holiness and righteousness.

Divisions of the Building

The tabernacle's three sections each had a special significance, showing the movement of man toward God.

The outer court. This was the only place where the average Israelite could go. Here the priests offered sacrifices for the people on the brazen altar. The fact that it was without a covering teaches us that all things we do are open to the gaze of God.

The outer court teaches other truths about our relationship with God. The curtains around it, 7½ feet high, taught that man was excluded from God because of sin. But the wall was of cloth, teaching that the separation was temporary. And the doorway into the outer court taught that God had made a way whereby man could approach Him.

The Holy Place. As the outer court revealed the way to God, the Holy Place represented service for God. There were three items in this section of the tabernacle. The golden candlestick taught the need for testimony; the table of showbread typified spiritual nourishment and fellowship; and the golden altar of incense typified worship and intercession.

The Holy of Holies. Here was God's special dwelling place. The veil that separated it from the Holy Place showed that perfect communion with God and perfect access to Him were not yet possible. The ark, which contained the tablets of the Law, taught the justice of God. On the other hand, the mercy seat, which served as a crown for the ark, taught that a just God can also be merciful, when the blood of atonement has been shed. We'll talk more about these parts of the tabernacle later.

The Tabernacle Was a "Prophet"

In a sense, types are prophetic, for they demonstrated what God would do in the future.

Through the tabernacle, God had found a way to have fellowship and communion with His people. This was prophetic of the time when He would provide a way to have perfect union and communion with mankind. When was this? When His Son "tabernacled" (that's the meaning of the word *dwelt* in John 1:14) among men. Jesus was the means by which God could reveal himself to men.

But the "prophecy" of the tabernacle went even further than the ministry of Jesus on earth. God now dwells in a *spiritual* temple, the Church. Also, every individual member of the body of Christ is a temple, a means by which God can reveal himself to the world. So the tabernacle was a preview of Christ, of the Church, and of the believer.

The Boundary of the Building

At this point, let's consider what is meant by a "cubit," the basic unit of measurement used in constructing the tabernacle.

How far is it from the tip of your elbow to the tip of your middle finger? It varies, of course, according to the size of the man, but that was a common method of measuring distance in ancient times. (It was good to have a tall slave, for his "cubit" would be longer than that of a shorter man.)

For an easy method of measuring, think of the cubit as 18 inches. (Most Bible students use this measurement.) So multiply all cubit distances by 1½. For example, the length of the outer court was 100 cubits, or 150 feet; the breadth 50 cubits, or 75 feet.

In your imagination, walk around the outer court. You'll see a "fence" made of white linen—5 cubits (7½ feet) high. It was supported by 20 brazen pillars on each side and 10 on each end. The pillars were connected by silver rods.

Purity Personified

The cloth of the curtain was made from flax. Its snowy whiteness typified the purity and righteousness of Jesus Christ, the spotless Son of God.

Neither the enemies nor the friends of Jesus could find fault with Him. Pilate could find no fault in Him. Judas confessed he had betrayed innocent blood (Matthew 27:4). And Peter, who was closely associated with our Lord, said He "did no sin, neither was guile found in his mouth" (1 Peter 2:22).

Excluded but Welcome

The curtain kept everyone outside the tabernacle. Because it was 7½ feet high, no one could see over it (not many men are 8 feet tall); and they couldn't see under it or through it. They had to come through the door. And there was only one door. The curtain reminds us of what Jesus said to Nicodemus: "Except a man be born again, he cannot see the kingdom of God" (John 3:3).

A perfect square. The distance between the pillars was 5 cubits (7½ feet), the same as the height of the curtain, so between each pillar there was a perfect square. This reminds me of the four-sided view of Christ we see in the Gospels, with each emphasizing a different aspect of Jesus' ministry—King, Servant, Man, and God.

Special Supports

The tabernacle and its outer court faced eastward. Get the picture in your mind again. The 7½-feet high curtains were suspended on pillars of brass—20 on the north, 20 on the south, and 10 on the east and the west respectively. Four of the eastern pillars were used as a doorway into the outer court.

Fillets (pronounce them the way they're spelled, including the "t"), referred to in Exodus 27:11, were silver connecting rods, many think, between the pillars. They supported the pillars and helped them bear the weight of the curtain. The pillars and their bases were made of brass. Each contained a silver hook on which the curtain was hung.

A beautiful picture. Brass typifies God's justice, and the white linen curtains represent Christ's righteousness imparted to us (1 Corinthians 1:30). It is not of our own doing.

A pillar or a pillow? Some believers are like pillows, too soft to be of much good. Others, as God intends, are pillars, able to bear a burden.

Burden-bearers—that's what God is looking for. According to Galatians 6:5, each believer should bear his own burden. But that's not enough. As verse 2 states, we should bear the burdens of others too.

The pillars could not stand alone, they were placed in brass sockets. If we are to be pillars in the Church, we cannot stand in our own strength. What is the source of our enablement? "Be strong in the Lord, and in the power of his might" (Ephesians 6:10).

The Door of the Building

"One door and only one, and yet its sides are two; inside and outside, on which side are you?" Remember the little children singing that? A simple message but a profound truth.

There was only one way to get inside the outer court, and from there to the tabernacle proper. It's easy to understand that point, isn't it?

God has always had a way by which men could draw near to Him—but only one way. Noah's ark, a type of salvation, had only one door. In John 14:6, when Jesus was talking with His disciples, the Master said, "I am the way." Not one of the ways, along with Confucius, Buddha, or Muhammad. *The* Way.

Later, Peter boldly declared to the high priest: "Neither is there salvation in any other: for there is none other name under heaven given among men, whereby we must be saved" (Acts 4:12).

Picturing the Gospels

In chapter 1 of this book you learned the meaning of various colors used in the Scriptures. Here, like a rainbow, we see them mingled in the beautiful door to the outer court. They remind us of the ministry of Jesus and His nature, as presented in the four Gospels.

There was *purple*, meaning royalty. This shows Christ the King, as revealed in the Gospel of Matthew.

There was *scarlet*, which spoke of Christ the perfect Servant, as revealed in the Gospel of Mark.

There was *white linen*. It spoke of Christ, the perfect Man, as revealed in the Gospel of Luke.

Finally, there was a lovely *blue*, the heavenly color, speaking of the Gospel of John, where Jesus is revealed as the Son of God.

What a message the door presents! It was the only way to forgiveness, but it was wide enough—30 feet—so only those who refused to enter remained outside.

6
Provision for Cleansing

Don't be worried if you don't understand every detail of the tabernacle. Join the club. We don't either.

It's something like a parable, which is meant to teach one major truth. If you try to stress the details, you can get way off base—and miss the major truths the Scriptures are trying to teach you.

It really doesn't matter too much if we don't understand the meaning of such things as the fleshhooks, the network of brass, etc. Actually, they may not mean anything at all. Just leave the technical aspects to Bezaleel, the architect and construction engineer who worked with Moses.

Now we have reached the outer court. Two objects call for our attention—the brazen altar and the brazen laver.

The Place of Sacrifice

As an Israelite walked into the outer court, his eyes immediately fell on the brazen altar. He could go no farther until he had done what was necessary at this altar. Here all the sacrifices were offered. God has always insisted that man can come to Him only by means of a sacrifice.

Description of the altar. The brazen altar was made of acacia wood (the most durable wood available) covered with brass, as were the poles used for carrying the altar. (Throughout, brass means copper.) It was 5 cubits (7½ feet) each way and 4½ feet high.

Why Have Sacrifices? An Altar?

How can man who is innately sinful approach a God who is intrinsically holy? Only one way. The sin must be eliminated. How? By a sacrifice. That's the reason for the altar.

The fire. After the tabernacle had been erected, the priesthood established, and everything in order, the first sacrifices were placed on the altar (Leviticus 9). Then a miraculous event took place. According to verse 24: "There came a fire out from before the Lord, and consumed upon the altar the burnt offering and the fat."

Kindled by a divine act, this fire was never to be allowed to go out. Tradition tells us that the sacred fire was maintained until the people of God went into Babylonian captivity many centuries later.

The method of sacrifice. Before an animal was slain as an offering for sin, the guilty person placed his hand on the head of the animal, by faith transferring his guilt. Then the beast was killed and burned on the altar.

It's easy to see the meaning of this, isn't it? The brazen altar is a picture of Calvary. The animal was the substitute for the sinner, who needed to be judged. The beast took the man's place.

Jesus was the "Lamb of God, which taketh away the sin of the world" (John 1:29). When we come as sinners, by faith we can place our sins upon Him, believing in faith that He died for us on the cross. He is the great Substitute who died that all might live.

A sacred place. The word *altar* means "high place," "lifted up." The brazen altar typifies the cross on which Jesus was placed. This is what Jesus meant when He said: "And I, if I be lifted up from the earth, will draw all men unto me" (12:32).

The altar was a place for the shedding of blood. Located outside the tabernacle, it proclaimed by its very position that a blood sacrifice is needed before there can be communion with God. "Without shedding of blood is no remission" (Hebrews 9:22).

The altar was a place of substitution. An Israelite who had sinned could offer an animal to die in his place as a substitute. That's the meaning of Leviticus 1:4 "He shall put his hand upon the head of the burnt offering; and it shall be accepted for him to make atonement for him."

What a beautiful picture of Calvary! On the cross, Jesus was our Substitute. By rights, you and I belonged there, but Jesus took our place.

A Picture of the Incarnation

The materials the brazen altar was made from represent the humanity of the Son of God who became the Son of Man—for one reason, that He might die for us.

This altar of sacrifice was made of acacia wood, from a tree that grew in the desert (the King James Version refers to it as shittim wood). The wood was white and very durable.

Wood often symbolizes humanity and is a picture of Jesus' human nature. The Incarnation was necessary so there could be Redemption. If Christ had remained in heaven He couldn't have died for us. He had to be born so He could die.

Humanity judged. The wood of the brazen altar represents humanity, and the brass placed over the wood represents judgment.

Do you see what all this means? All mankind has sinned and deserves judgment, for a holy God cannot tolerate sin. By becoming man Jesus identified himself with the human race, all of whom were under the curse. On the cross, the judgment all of us deserved covered the wood of Jesus' humanity.

Those who take Jesus as Saviour will never need to suffer judgment for their sins, since Jesus has already suffered it for them. "There is therefore now no condemnation [judgment] to them which are in Christ Jesus" (Romans 8:1).

Good News

Journalists have said the word *news* represents the four major directions of the compass—north, east, west, and south. The four horns, one on each corner of the brazen altar, shouted the greatest newsstory of all time. Pointing toward the four corners of the earth, they proclaimed the fact that the salvation of Jesus Christ would be for everybody, everywhere.

Plenty of Room at the Cross

Of the seven pieces of furniture found in the outer court and the tabernacle proper, the brazen altar was the largest; big enough, in fact, to hold the other six pieces.

What a picture of God's provision in Redemption! Salvation includes all the blessings and privileges any of us will ever need. Paul proclaimed this: "He that spared not his own Son, but delivered him up for us all, how shall he not with him also freely give us all things?" (v. 32).

The Ascension. As the smoke of the sacrifices rose toward heaven, it symbolized God's acceptance of the offering. It also typified Jesus' ascension and the Father's acceptance of the Calvary sacrifice. Because of this our Saviour now stands before the throne of God as our Mediator, interceding for us.

The Atonement. After an animal had been killed as an atonement and part of the blood sprinkled on the altar, the rest was poured out at the base. It reminds us of the great old song: "There is a fountain filled with blood, drawn from Immanuel's veins, and sinners plunged beneath that flood lose all their guilty stains."

A Place to Get Clean

The average Israelite needed only the brazen altar. When he had brought an animal to be sacrificed and atonement had been made for his sins, his obligation was over.

But the Levites were a unique breed. The tribe of Levi had been chosen for a special purpose. God had selected them to serve Him in the tabernacle. They were the priests of Israel. There was work for them to do inside the tabernacle. (In the Holy Place, that is. Not the Holy of Holies. Only one man could go in there, the high priest. We'll come to him later.) The brazen laver teaches one great big truth—before service there must be cleansing.

The laver symbolized sacrifice of a very special kind. Exodus 38:8 tells us the women of the congregation of Israel gave their mirrors, made of brass in those days, for the making of this item. There were no mirrors of glass in those ancient days. They were made of polished brass, probably beautiful specimens of Egyptian handcraft. If you should ever visit the famous museum at Cairo, Egypt, you will be able to see similar mirrors there.

What did the laver look like? That's an unanswerable question. The Bible tells us nothing about its shape or its size. It must have had a large base so it would stand up easily. It was never covered.

Cleaning the Cleansed

We see two great truths in the brazen laver: (1) we need to be cleansed; and (2) there's a way to get clean. As a priest drew near the laver, because it was made of polished brass, he could clearly see himself and observe his need for cleansing. But more than that, there was water in the laver. Not only could he see his need, a way had been provided whereby he could get clean before going inside the Holy Place to serve.

A fresh cleansing. The sacrifice at the brazen altar had atoned for the sins of the priest, but in walking from the altar to the laver on his way to the door of the tabernacle he had soiled his feet, as the dust sifted through his open sandals.

Before entering the tabernacle itself, God's dwelling place, the priest needed to make sure he was clean. This wasn't an optional matter. There was no alternative. God had commanded it.

Daily cleansing. You and I have been made priests unto God. After salvation comes service. The brazen altar represents the cross of Christ, where He cleansed our lives by His blood from the sins of the past. The brazen laver represents the daily cleansing necessary to keep us clean.

Not dirty, but soiled. Why do you like to take a shower or a bath at the close of a long, hard day? Looking at yourself casually, you can't see any dirt on yourself. But you know there is dust in the air which attaches itself to our bodies without our knowing it. When you look at the water after taking a bath, you're glad you did.

Our daily activities, as we come in contact with worldly influences, may be likened to dust. We may not have sinned or be conscious of having done anything wrong, but as the poet said, "The world is too much with us." Sin has an unconscious influence on us.

That's why we need daily cleansing. *Dust will become dirt.*

Jesus illustrated this perfectly in the Upper Room. John describes the scene in the 13th chapter of his Gospel. You know the scene well. Jesus found it necessary to wash the disciples' feet as a demonstration of humility. None of the men had been willing to do this menial task—they'd been too busy arguing about who would be greatest in the Kingdom.

You see, in those days they often had public baths. But after bathing there, people had to walk with their open sandals through the dusty streets to their homes. So the custom was to have a slave whose duty it was to bathe the feet of guests. Jesus referred to this practice later when He said: "He that is washed needeth not save to wash his feet, but is clean every whit" (v. 10).

We have been to the great public bath—Calvary. We have been cleansed. But day by day, we come in contact with contaminations as we associate with unbelievers in necessary contacts. Daily contacts like this call for daily cleansing. That's the message of the laver.

A Wonderful Laver

What is our laver? The Word of God. Ephesians 5:25,26 affirms: "Christ . . . loved the church, and gave himself for it; that he might sanctify and cleanse it with the washing of water by the word." And Jesus himself said: "Now ye are clean through the word which I have spoken unto you" (John 15:3).

Have you ever noticed that the Bible is like a mirror? As you read its pages and meditate on its truths, suddenly you find it describing your own condition.

The Holy Spirit, the divine Author, is also the Interpreter. As we read the Bible and consider what it says, He applies it to our particular needs. It is "quick, and powerful, and sharper than any two-edged sword," and He makes it to be "a discerner of the thoughts and intents of the heart" (Hebrews 4:12).

Like the laver, the Word serves as a mirror to show us our need of cleansing; then as we immerse ourselves in the Word, it cleanses us. That's what David meant when he said: "Wherewithal shall a young man cleanse his way? By taking heed thereto according to thy word" (Psalm 119:9).

Something Else to Clean Us Up

The Word cleanses us—but that's not all. The blood of Jesus Christ not only cleanses us at salvation, it also cleanses us day by day.

Notice carefully what 1 John 1:7 says: "The blood of Jesus Christ his Son cleanseth us from all sin." The verb *cleanseth* is in the continuous present, not the past tense. Sometimes this verse is used as an evangelistic text for sinners, and I suppose that's all right. But John was writing to *believers*. It's a promise Christians can claim.

Believers Need Brass

Not the kind usually thought of in connection with a person who is too forward and cocky. Brass, remember, speaks of judgment, and believers need a special kind.

I'm talking about *self*-judgment. We should not wait for others to find failures in our Christian conduct. We should be the first to discover those flaws.

Periodically, churches celebrate the Lord's Supper, usually once a month. In 1 Corinthians 11 Paul points out the opportunity this gives us to search our lives and see if we measure up to God's standards of holiness. What should we do if we find that which is displeasing to God? The answer is simple. Bring those sins and failures to the Cross.

There is a golden opportunity at each Communion service. Paul points out further in verses 31 and 32 that by judging our sins and getting our lives cleansed, we are saving ourselves from facing them at the judgment. God must judge sin. We can cooperate with Him, so we will not have to be condemned with the unbelievers.

Visit the laver every day!

7
When Divine and Human Meet

The "testimony" of the boards. In his book *Simple Talks on the Tabernacle* D. H. Dolman tells a very beautiful parable about the boards used for the sides of the tabernacle. Listen while the board "testifies":

"At one time I was an acacia tree in the desert. I grew out of it. All my nourishment I got from the earth. God had cursed the earth. As long as I was rooted in the desert, I could not possibly have a place in the tabernacle. I had necessarily to be taken out of the desert soil, from which I drew all my nourishment.

"One day a stranger came, his name was Bezaleel. He looked at me and at the other trees near me. Then he came back and smiled.... I found out he had chosen me for a board in the tabernacle. Why he chose me and not the others I really cannot tell. I feel sure I was not any better than the others....

"Then came a day I shall never forget. A man came with a strong axe and put it to my roots. Blow after blow fell. At last I fell and died. I had to be separated entirely from the desert life. that was necessary.

"Do not think I was ready now for a board in the tabernacle. God took a great deal of pains with me ... I had to be planed. That was necessary again. I should not have fitted into my place otherwise.... There was so much of my old nature which would never have fitted in the tabernacle. . . .

"You want to know what happened to me then? The Master did put me again in the desert, but this time it was all different. It had all become new. In fact, I have become a new creature. Something has happened inside of me and outside as well. I do not belong any more to the desert. . . . I am standing in two silver sockets. I like to call them grace and truth. The sockets stand between me and the desert. . . . I am not alone anymore. There are other boards on either side of me, and we are so closely united together that we form one solid wall—all one in Christ Jesus. Look at me, you see that I am different. Do you know me still? You cannot see my wood at all. I am overlaid with gold."*

A Mobile Church

Since the people of Israel were living in the wilderness and frequently had to move, the structure that was their center of worship had to be designed so it could be put up or taken down quickly.

It wasn't very large, but what the tabernacle lacked in size, it made up for in grandeur. In one sense the outer court was a part of the tabernacle, but now we're going to look at the building itself.

Let's remind ourselves of the tabernacle's dimensions—45 feet long, 15 feet wide, and 15 feet high. It was sort of a tent—easy to take down, to carry, and to put up.

It was quite a demonstration of organization when the tabernacle was taken down as the Israelites got

---

*D. H. Dolman, *Simple Talks on the Tabernacle* (Grand Rapids, Michigan: Zondervan Publishing Company, 1941). Used by permission.

ready to move to a new place of encampment. Numbers 4 tells about it. Each of the three family groups of the Levites had a specific task to perform. Since there were 22,000 Levites, according to verse 39 (though many were children), there were enough workmen to do the job fast.

Now back to the structure of the tabernacle. (You might want to read the details in Exodus 26.) It was sort of a tent, but it wasn't supported by a tent pole as tents are today. There was a framework of wood consisting of 48 boards, each 15 feet feet high and 27 inches wide. On the south and north sides there were 20 boards each, plus 6 boards at the west end, with 2 boards for the corners. Each board was set into a solid block of silver to keep it standing firmly.

To hold the boards together, there were 5 bars: two at the top, each running halfway; two at the bottom, each also running halfway; then a middle bar that went from one end to the other. The roof consisted of 4 kinds of curtains, each a different color. They went across the top and hung down on the north, south, and west sides.

The Glory Boards

D. H. Dolman's parable of the boards introduces us to the meaning of this part of the tabernacle. The boards are a type of Christ and of individual believers. United, they typify the Church, which is composed of all born-again followers of the Lord.

Now, let's look at the boards in detail. The acacia tree of the desert was not very large, so probably one tree was needed for each board (remember, they were 15 feet high). They had to be cut and shaped so they would fit with the other boards and form a solid structure.

Since the boards were covered with gold, no one could tell their humble background.

They are a picture of Jesus. The wood represents humanity, the gold deity. An illustration of the combination of the human and divine found in Christ—the Son of Man and the Son of God.

Jesus was human. Isaiah prophesied of Him: "He shall grow up before him as a tender plant, and as a root out of a dry ground" (Isaiah 53:2). There was nothing in Jesus' background that would make people think of Him as the Son of God. His own townspeople asked, "Is not this the son of the carpenter?" Even His own brothers didn't believe on Him at first.

Jesus was (and is) divine. Most of the time while He was on earth, people saw only His humanity. But after His resurrection and ascension, He once more assumed the place of deity that belonged to Him. It was as a man that Jesus ascended. Now in the glory world, His deity and glory cover His humanity.

They picture believers. Bezaleel, the great architect of the tabernacle, was a type of the Holy Spirit. He chose the trees from which the boards were made. He supervised the making of the boards into suitable parts of the tabernacle. Just so, the Holy Spirit today chooses men and women and works with them, fitting them into the Church.

We too are "roots out of a dry ground." In our first birth we received a human nature, with all its weaknesses and failings. But Peter tells us we have been made "partakers of the divine nature" (2 Peter 1:4). The glory of God's nature covers the wood of our human nature. Be sure to keep the wood hidden and let the gold shine!

The silver of Redemption. Each socket helping to support a board was 16 inches long and weighed about 100 pounds. Two sockets were under each board. All the sockets fitted together in such a way that they gave the appearance of a solid silver foundation.

The source of the silver provides a clue to the meaning of the sockets. It came from the redemption money paid by the male Israelites when they were numbered in the census. So silver signifies Redemption. Peter tells us: "Ye know that ye were not redeemed with corruptible things, as silver and gold, . . . but with the precious blood of Christ, as of a lamb without blemish and without spot" (1 Peter 1:18,19).

The sockets kept the boards from falling. A simple statement, but think what it means. The same power that redeemed us can also keep us. If we trust in our own strength, we will fail, but if we place our trust in Jesus, like Paul we shall be able to say: "I know whom I have believed, and am persuaded that he is able to keep that which I have committed unto him against that day" (2 Timothy 1:12).

We need the bars too. They held the boards together. What is it that helps us maintain our Christian fellowship? Our common faith in Christ. Our fellowship with other Christians. Attending the house of God. And the bar that passed through all the boards, important though unseen, speaks of the work of the Holy Spirit, who creates an invisible union and makes us one fellowship, one brotherhood.

Beautiful Pictures of Jesus

The coverings of the tabernacle are four pictures of Jesus—His nature, His character, His ministry, and His atonement.

The four coverings formed the roof of the tabernacle and hung down on three sides. (The eastern side of the tabernacle had a special door, which we'll examine in detail later.)

Remember again the dimensions of the tabernacle, so you can picture the function of the coverings. It was 45 feet long, 15 feet wide, and 15 feet high. Three of the four coverings were 60 feet long (made of 10 curtains, each 6 feet wide). So they could reach the length of the tabernacle, then hang down the 15 feet at the back.

Crosswise of the tabernacle, three of the coverings were 42 feet long, so they covered the top of the tabernacle (15 feet) and hung down to within 1½ feet of the ground on either side.

A special covering. The one made of goats' hair was 66 feet long, instead of 60 (11 curtains instead of 10). Also, it stretched 45 feet across, instead of 42 feet, so it hung all the way to the ground on either side. I'll tell you why later.

A Saviour Who Served

The badgers' skin covering. This was on top; the one seen by outsiders. It was probably a very dark-blue material, almost black, and tanned like leather. It wasn't very beautiful, but it was very useful, protecting the tabernacle from the weather.

Here is a picture of Jesus the Servant. The prophet said of Him: "When we shall see him, there is no beauty that we should desire him" (Isaiah 53:2). Oh, it's true that Jesus brought joy to others when He lived on earth. But He found little in His everyday existence to bring happiness to himself. He was a man of sorrows and acquainted with grief, despised, rejected, homeless, and poor. And when He hung on Calvary it wasn't a pretty sight.

Why did Jesus endure all this? Because His purpose was to minister to others. Listen as He tells His disciples: "Even the Son of man came not to be ministered unto, but to minister, and to give his life a ransom for many" (Mark 10:45). He humbled himself that others might be exalted.

The badgers' skin covering speaks of Jesus' humiliation and humble service.

A Saviour Who Suffered

The rams' skin covering. This was just beneath the badgers' skin covering—skins of rams, dyed red.

What does a ram picture? It was a ceremonially clean animal that was sacrificed when priests were consecrated for service in their sacred office. So it speaks of suffering.

How very much Jesus suffered! It was the only way He could accomplish our salvation—taking our punishment, dying our death. When Abraham was about to offer Isaac on Mt. Moriah, God intervened and provided a sacrifice. Isaac was spared, but not Jesus.

Think of the agony of Gethsemane and the torturous hours on Calvary. Jesus fulfilled Isaiah's prophecy: "I gave my back to the smiters, and my cheeks to them that plucked off the hair: I hid not my face from shame and spitting" (Isaiah 50:6).

A Saviour Who Was a Substitute

The goats' hair covering. This was longer than the other three, containing an extra 6-foot panel. This extra curtain was doubled and hung over the front of the tabernacle as a 3-foot valance. The doubled curtain has a beautiful meaning which we will look at later.

Most of the goats in the Middle East are small and with black hair. However, some breeds have fine, white silky hair, and many students believe this was the kind chosen for the tabernacle covering. The 1½ feet that extended beyond the other coverings provided a beautiful white border.

What does the covering of goats' hair represent? It probably has reference to what happened on the Day of Atonement once a year, when the high priest offered a sacrifice for the sins of the entire nation.

Two goats were brought before the Lord on that day. The priest cast lots, and one goat was chosen to be offered as a sin offering. Its blood was brought into the Holy of Holies (where the high priest could come only once a year) and sprinkled on the mercy seat which covered the ark of the covenant. Within the ark were the two tablets of stone on which God himself had written the Ten Commandments—which later the Israelites had disobeyed. So the blood on the mercy seat pictured the mercy of God in covering the broken Law and forgiving His people.

The other animal was called the scapegoat. It was brought to the brazen altar. Laying his hands on the head of the scapegoat, the high priest recited the sins of the people, in a sense transferring their sins to the animal, their substitute. Then the goat was led away, never to return to the camp.

Jesus' work of redemption is so great, it takes the two animals to picture it. As our Sin Offering, Jesus paid the price of our sins by His shed blood. But also (isn't it glorious?) He carried our sins so far away, they can never be brought back again.

Now the doubled curtain! At one time in Eastern countries when a bill had been paid, the paper or parchment was folded double and a nail was driven through it. Everyone who saw it knew the debt had been paid.

The doubled goats' hair curtain proclaims the news: "Jesus paid it all." That's what happened when the nails fastened Jesus to the cross.

A Saviour Who Was Spotless

The fine-twined linen curtain. This was the most beautiful covering of all. To see it one had to go beyond the outer court and into the Holy Place. Those who had to stay outside saw only the dark-blue badgers' skins. But inside, the priests saw the golden walls and a ceiling with beautiful embroidery, shining and reflecting the light from the 7-pronged candlestick.

This curtain was woven with blue, purple, and scarlet thread, picturing cherubim, angelic figures. The white signifies the purity, righteousness, and holiness of Jesus; the blue, His heavenly nature; the purple, His royalty and omnipotence; and the scarlet, His suffering and atonement.

A closing caution: Don't be content with being an "outer-court Christian," just satisfied with being saved. We are called to be priests unto God, ministering for Him. There you will find beauties in Redemption the ordinary Christian cannot know.

8
A Special Place for Special People

After an old sea captain found the Lord as his Saviour he used an unusual way to testify. He taught his parrot to say, "Come in," when people knocked; then, "Are you converted? If you are, it's all right."

Compared to the way sinners live, salvation certainly is all right—but it's not the end, it's just the beginning. The outer court, with its typical meaning, is wonderful, but we can't afford to stay there. Let's go on and see what God wants for us.

In his book *Typical Truths in the Tabernacle*, W. S. Hottel speaks of the seven steps an Israelite had to take to go from the wilderness to the Holy of Holies: (1) *Decision* at the gate; (2) *Acceptance* at the brazen altar; (3) *Cleansing* at the brazen laver; (4) *Intercession* at the golden altar of incense; (5) *Fellowship* at the table of showbread; (6) *Testimony* at the golden candlestick; and (7) *Faith turned to sight* within the veil in the Holy of Holies.

Lights in the World—Shine!

God did not want His sanctuary to be lit by natural light. "The natural man receiveth not the things of the Spirit of God: for they are foolishness unto him: neither can he know them, because they are spiritually discerned" (1 Corinthians 2:14).

In the Holy Place God planned to have a special light, from the golden candlestick. It represents your testimony as a believer. Its message to you is, "Shine!"

Jesus is the golden candlestick. He said of himself, "I am the light of the World" (John 8:12). "In him was life; and the life was the light of men" (1:4). And Revelation 21:23 tells us He will be the light of the celestial city.

But *you* are part of that golden candlestick too. We might say that Jesus is the main shaft and believers are the branches. It's sort of like the Parable of the Vine and the Branches in John 15. But you're of no use without the main shaft of the candlestick. Notice there are only six branches, one short of the perfect number. Have you noticed also that the main shaft stands higher than the branches? Why not? We always knew, didn't we, that Jesus is the Head of the Church.

The Holy Place was supremely beautiful. Try to imagine its loveliness. It wasn't very large, only 30 feet by 15 feet, but the soft glow of the candlestick was reflected by the gold-covered boards that formed the sides of the tabernacle. And the light illuminated the beautiful, many-colored embroidery work of the ceiling.

However, without the light from the candlestick, no one could see all that loveliness. No wonder God's first words recorded in the Bible were: "Let there be light." No wonder one of the first things Jesus said to His followers was: "Let your light . . . shine."

Suffering comes before shining. The candlestick was made of beaten gold. Laid on an anvil, it received blow upon blow, until it was wafer thin. Then it was folded over upon itself and beaten again.

The torturing blows of the hammer had a purpose. They caused the loose crystalline pattern of the raw material to be forced into a new, tight, uniform, and fibrous grainy structure. This produced the ability to withstand strain, along with a tough flexibility.

It was this process that produced the famous "Toledo blade" made in Spain, the best sword in the world of its time. The blacksmith would take a hot piece of fine steel and beat it out to a thin strip. Then folding it over upon itself, he would beat it out again and again, sometimes as much as 130 times. What a beating that blade took, but in combat it could literally cut a lesser blade in half.

Suffering before service is a principle of life. The beating of the gold for the candlestick typifies the suffering Jesus endured to come to the place of glory He now occupies.

Are we any better than our Lord? It's all right to aspire to being a part of the candlestick, to want to shine along with Him. But if we want to share in the glory we must be willing to share in the bruising that produces the glory.

Oil Makes the Light Shine

Oil was the one important ingredient. Without it, there could be no light. The main purpose of the candlestick was not to be beautiful but to provide light. Even Jesus, in His earthly ministry, depended on the oil of the Holy Spirit to perform His miracles. "God anointed Jesus of Nazareth with the Holy Ghost and with power: who went about doing good, and healing all that were oppressed of the devil; for God was with him" (Acts 10:38).

If Jesus needed the oil of the Holy Spirit to fulfill His ministry, don't you think *you* do?

Once isn't enough. A man once said to a fellow believer, "I'll be so glad when I get the Baptism, so I won't have to seek anymore." Poor fellow! He knew very little about the meaning of the Baptism. It is just the beginning. To think one filling is enough is as silly as filling the gas tank with 20 gallons of gasoline and expecting it to last for a 1,000-mile trip!

The candlestick needed constant care. The oil had to be replenished. The wicks had to be trimmed. The wicks, soaked with the oil, were the means by which the light was shed abroad.

Our talents and abilities are like the wicks. But the wicks were not to call attention to themselves. God did not want people to say, "Oh, what beautiful wicks," but rather to admire the candlestick. Since Jesus is the candlestick, what does that say to you?

Sometimes the priest had to trim the wicks so they would burn brighter. Have you ever had your wick trimmed?

Communion With Christ—Eat!

Size isn't everything. The table of showbread (literally "Bread of the Presence") was quite small—3 feet long, 18 inches wide, and 27 inches high. Like the boards of the tabernacle, it was made of acacia wood covered with gold.

By the way, notice that brass was the dominant metal in the outer court, while gold was the metal used in the Holy Place. There must be judgment on sin (represented by the brass) before the divine glory (represented by the gold) can be seen.

Each week 12 loaves of unleavened bread were baked and set on the table of showbread in 2 rows, 6 in each row. The old loaves were then eaten by the priest in the Holy Place.

Each of the 12 loaves represented one of the tribes of Israel. Notice too that frankincense was put on the bread "for a memorial" (Leviticus 24:7). This teaches us that God never forgets His people. "He hath said, I will never leave thee, nor forsake thee" (Hebrews 13:5). Always there were some of these loaves on the table, continually proclaiming the truth that God remembers.

Jesus the Bread of Life

The table of showbread had a number of typical meanings. For example, the loaves are a type of Christ. He himself said: "I am that bread of life. . . . Except ye eat the flesh of the Son of man, and drink his blood, ye have no life in you" (John 6:48,53).

Bread has a beautiful symbolism. Bread comes from grain which must first fall into the ground and die. Then it springs up to a new, better life. In so doing, it pictures the death, burial, and resurrection of the Son of God. The grinding of the grain to make flour speaks of being made perfect through suffering. Only because Jesus was willing to be crushed and bruised could He become for us the Bread of Life.

It has always seemed to me very appropriate that Jesus, the Bread of Life, was born in Bethlehem, which literally means "House of Bread."

As the message of the golden candlestick is, "Shine," so the message of the table of showbread is, "Eat." The table of showbread was not just a piece of furniture to be admired. The bread on the table was not there to decorate it. If the priests left the bread there it could not nourish them. They had to eat it to get help.

What a message for us. Many people admire Jesus as a great leader, orator, even prophet, but that's not enough. It takes more than appreciation. By fellowship with Him we must partake of Him and receive divine life. The Word of God is also a source of nourishment. If we would grow spiritually we must come—and eat!

We've Been Included

In Old Testament times, only the priests could eat the loaves that had been on the table of showbread. What a difference there is now! Every believer is a priest and is welcome at the table of his Father.

You feel unworthy? Mephibosheth did too. Second Samuel 9 tells his story. As a son of Jonathan and a near relative of King Saul, he was considered worthy of death according to the customs of those days. But for the sake of his father Jonathan, Mephibosheth was welcomed to the king's table.

You deserve to feel unworthy. Our sins merit death. But God has accepted us for Jesus' sake, and we are invited to sit at His table.

Intercession—Pray!

It was rather tiny, the golden altar of incense—1½ feet long, 1½ feet wide, and 3 feet high. Like the table of showbread, it was made from wood covered with gold. Around the top was a golden rim. At the 4 corners were horns, and on top a golden censer, on which burning coals were placed. Twice a day, in the morning and evening, the high priest would put incense on the coals, and the fragrance of the special incense would rise toward heaven and permeate the atmosphere of the Holy Place.

While the message of the golden candlestick is, "Shine!" and the message of the table of showbread is, "Eat!" the golden altar of incense proclaims the message, "Pray!"

Only the priests could go inside the Holy Place, and their major ministry was to be mediators between God and man. Christ is our High Priest, the great Mediator. But we're priests too. We too have the ministry of intercession. We can represent God to men, and also represent men to God.

Notice this was an altar, which is always a place of sacrifice. It teaches us that there is an element of sacrifice in all true prayer. Praying is not an easy task. It is significant that when the apostles chose the first deacons, the reason they gave was: "We will give ourselves continually to prayer, and to the ministry of the word" (Acts 6:4). Genuine prayer requires "giving" on our part—sacrificing some of our own ease and pleasure. But oh, the results!

Keep the Fire Burning

Keep fresh in your mind the meaning of the various items in the tabernacle and outer court, and you will obtain some beautiful truths. For example, the fire for the golden altar came from the brazen altar in the outer court. When we remember that the brazen altar represents Calvary, we learn that our approach to God (the golden altar—prayer) must always be on the basis of the Atonement. Only through the sacrifice of Christ can our prayers be effective.

Our Mediator. The golden altar reminds us of the work that Jesus, our High Priest, is now doing for us. Romans 8:34 tells us: "It is Christ that died, yea rather, that is risen again, who is even at the right hand of God, who also maketh intercession for us." No wonder we can expect our prayers to be answered—Jesus is praying for us too.

Want to be close to God? The piece of furniture in the Holy Place nearest the Holy of Holies was the golden altar. It stood just in front of the veil that led into the Holy of Holies, the place in the tabernacle where God manifested himself. What does this mean? There are many things we can do for God, but that which brings us closest to Him is the ministry of prayer and intercession.

Prayer Is a Fragrance

Twice a day the high priest came and stirred the coals of the fire on the golden altar till they glowed, and then he put incense on it. As the incense burned, it sent waves of fragrance throughout the Holy Place. As it arose, perfuming the atmosphere, it symbolized acceptance with God.

Revelation 8:3 tells of a similar scene: "Another angel came and stood at the altar, having a golden censer; and there was given unto him much incense, that he should offer it with the prayers of all saints upon the golden altar which was before the throne."

A special kind. The high priest could not use just any kind of incense. God himself had prescribed the ingredients—and they were to be used only for this purpose.

What are the ingredients that make our prayer life pleasing to God? Here are some: fervency, sincerity, submission, praise, and worship.

Twice a Day and All Day Long

The incense was burned on the golden altar at the time the morning and evening sacrifices were offered. David said: "Let my prayer be set forth before thee as incense; and the lifting up of my hands as the evening sacrifice" (Psalm 141:2).

When should we pray and how often? The golden altar gives a clue. When the incense was placed on the fire in the morning and in the evening, the flame flared and the perfume rose with it. But that wasn't all. Between times, the perfume from the smoldering incense continued to rise. It's good to have definite times of prayer and devotion to God, but there should also be a constant outgoing of our hearts to Him.

Once a year, on the Day of Atonement, something special happened to the golden altar. When an animal was killed and offered for the sins of the entire congregation, some of that blood was sprinkled on the horns of this altar. It's good to make sure the altar of our hearts is cleansed. Only the blood of Christ can make our prayers acceptable to God.

9
Into the Presence of God

Have you ever visited the Lincoln Memorial in Washington, D. C.? It is a moving experience for anyone who reveres the memory of the "Great Emancipator." Or perhaps you have visited the tomb of some other great world leader and remember the awe that seized you. If so, this gives you some idea of how the Israelite felt about the Holy of Holies in the tabernacle.

Actually, any sense of respect the thought of some great person inspires in us is very small in comparison with the reverence God's people felt for this place.

The people of Israel had a good reason for fear. They knew what had happened to the two sons of Aaron when they offered "strange fire" before the Lord. Nadab and Abihu perished as the genuine fire "from the Lord" consumed them.

Only one person among the hundreds of thousands of people in the ranks of the Israelites dared go into the Holy of Holies. And he was allowed to do this only once a year—on the Day of Atonement—with the blood of the animal that had been offered to atone for the sins of the whole nation.

Ancient historians tell us that it was the custom to attach a rope to the high priest on the Day of Atonement, so his body could be pulled out if by chance he should offend God and be killed.

The dimensions. The tabernacle proper, 45 feet long, was divided into two sections: the Holy Place, which was 30 feet long, and the Holy of Holies, which was 15 feet long. Since the height of the tabernacle was the same as the boards, 15 feet, and the width was the same distance, the Holy of Holies was a perfect cube, 15 feet long, wide, and high. Perhaps a reference to the Trinity.

The Throne Room of God

It was in the Holy of Holies that God manifested His presence. From that place ascended the pillar of fire and cloud. They were sometimes called the "Shekinah," which means the "Presence."

The Holy of Holies prefigured heaven. Comparing Christ with the high priest who entered into the Holy of Holies just once a year, the writer of Hebrews says: "For Christ is not entered into the holy places made with hands, which are the figures of the true; but into heaven itself, now to appear in the presence of God for us" (Hebrews 9:24).

Located at the west end of the tabernacle, the Holy of Holies was separated from the Holy Place by a beautiful veil. It contained two pieces of furniture that were separate but united—the ark of the covenant, and the mercy seat, which formed a lid or covering for the ark.

A Beautiful Doorway

Between the two parts of the tabernacle hung a veil. Like the bottom covering for the roof of the tabernacle, it was made of woven cloth (white linen) embroidered with cherubim in blue, purple, and scarlet colors.

The purpose of the veil. Primarily, the veil was a barrier. It silently said, "Stay out, under penalty of death." It prevented perfect fellowship between man and God. Remember, only one man, the high priest, could pass it and only once a year on the Day of Atonement.

Doesn't God want people to come to Him? Of course, He does. Well then, why this barrier? Actually, it shut God in. He's perfectly holy. As long as anyone has unforgiven sin in his life, he can't have fellowship with God. Sin always brings a barrier between God and man.

One encouraging word we can say about this veil. Though it was a barrier, at least it was a veil, not a wall. This hinted at the fact that the barrier was *temporary*. A time was coming when it would be eliminated. Also, it was not always closed. The fact that it was opened once a year suggested that a time was coming when it would be always open. And you and I are living in that day!

The material of the veil. Since we have looked at the meaning of the colors before, let's concentrate on the fine-twined linen.

Linen is a type of righteousness. "The fine linen is the righteousness of saints" (Revelation 19:8). And since any righteousness we have comes from Christ who "is made unto us . . . righteousness" (1 Corinthians 1:30), it refers to Jesus' righteousness too. Jesus was completely righteous. "Thou hast loved righteousness, and hated iniquity" (Hebrews 1:9).

The word *fine* refers to Jesus' spotless innocence and faultlessness. He "did no sin, neither was guile found in his mouth" (1 Peter 2:22). The word *twined* conveys a beautiful thought. It pictures the Incarnation, the union of the divine and human in one Person. Jesus was perfectly human, the Son of Man. He possessed feelings and desires like any other man. But he was also perfectly divine. In Him, as in the Father, were the wisdom, knowledge, holiness, and power of Deity.

The Way Is Open!

We're not kept out anymore. We can go inside! How did it happen? By the death of the Son of God on the cross.

The veil represents the body of Christ. When He died, the veil of the temple was torn in two (Matthew 27:51). Hebrews 10:19, 20 describes the meaning: "Having therefore, brethren, boldness to enter into the holiest by the blood of Jesus, by a new and living way, which he hath consecrated for us, through the veil, that is to say, his flesh."

Because the body of our Lord was torn by the nails, the spear, and the thorns, the veil holding back men from the presence of God was also torn. Notice it was from the top to the bottom: from the top—God did it; to the bottom—the sacrifice of Jesus did a complete work.

The rending of the veil was no accident. The veil was strong. Some Jewish historians have said it was about 4 inches thick, and two yoke of oxen could not have torn it apart. Jesus had become what He proclaimed concerning himself: "I am the way" (John 14:6).

The Very Presence of God

Inside the Holy of Holies was the ark of the covenant, covered by a gold lid called the mercy seat. The ark was a box or chest, rectangular in shape, made of acacia wood and covered with gold. It was 45 inches long, 27 inches wide, and 27 inches high. Not really very large was it? But oh, the significance! The ark also had four rings of gold, two on each side, and staves by which it could be carried by the Levites.

The ark of the covenant was the piece of furniture that was made first. Then the other pieces were made, beginning with the Holy of Holies, out through the Holy

Place, then to the outer court, and ending with the brazen altar. The meaning of this? When man tries to reach God, he starts from the outside. But God begins from within. This also speaks of the initiative of God. In accomplishing Redemption, God didn't wait for man to come to Him; He moved toward man.

A visible sign of the invisible. Without question, the ark of the covenant typified the presence of God. Moses once prayed: "If thy presence go not with me, carry us not up hence" (Exodus 33:15). The ark proved God had answered Moses' prayer. Here, between the cherubim of the mercy seat, the God who is everywhere localized himself. From this place in the tabernacle, the pillar of fire by night and the pillar of cloud by day billowed up above the camp of Israel.

Because Jesus on earth was the visible presence of God, the ark typifies Him too. Both were a visible representation of God. God said of the tabernacle: "There I will meet with thee" (Exodus 25:22). Christ also was the divine Meeting Place for God and man.

The purpose and use of the ark. Notice the many ways the ark typifies our Lord:

(1) From it, God communed with Moses, the leader of His people.

(2) It symbolized guidance. "And they departed from the mount of the Lord three days' journey: and the ark of the covenant of the Lord went before them in the three days' journey, to search out a resting place for them" (Numbers 10:33).

(3) The ark symbolized victory. At Jericho it led the way, carried by the Levites, while the people of Israel marched around the walls.

(4) The ark symbolized divine leadership. When Israel was about to cross over the Jordan River into Canaan, the priests went first, carrying the ark. And when their

feet touched the water, the Jordan became a wall of water, and the people of Israel marched over on dry ground (Joshua 3:14-17).

What a picture of Jesus! It is through Him that God's blessings and revelations come. It is He who provides guidance for His people. To change the metaphor: "When he putteth forth his own sheep, he goeth before them" (John 10:4). He not only brings victory; He *is* our Victory. And He is the One who leads us past all difficulties into the Promised Land of His blessing.

The Contents Are Important

The ark of the covenant contained three items: (1) the two tablets of the Law; (2) a golden pot containing some of the manna with which God had fed His people in the wilderness; and (3) Aaron's rod, which had budded.

The tablets of the Law. The two pieces of stone containing the Ten Commandments were inside the ark. This was the second set, for Moses broke the first when he saw the sin into which Israel had fallen while he was on the mount. The unbroken tablets symbolize Jesus' perfect obedience. Never once did He fail to please the Father. He was without sin.

A golden pot of manna. "And Moses said unto Aaron, Take a pot, and put an omer full of manna therein, and lay it up before the Lord, to be kept for your generations" (Exodus 16:33).

The manna was to be a reminder to Israel of God's miraculous provision during the 40 years in the wilderness. It typified Jesus, the Living Bread. He told the Jews: "Your fathers did eat manna in the wilderness, and are dead. . . . I am the living bread which came down from heaven" (John 6:49,51). The pot of manna reminds us of God's promise to supply all our needs through Christ. Remember, the manna had to be gathered fresh each morning. We can't depend on yesterday's blessings for today's needs.

Aaron's rod that budded. This was a symbol of divine power. It had been used to bring the plagues upon Egypt, to make a path through the Red Sea, and to bring water out of the rock at Rephidim. And, held in the hand of Moses, it helped to bring victory over Amalek.

Perhaps the greatest victory using the rod came during Korah's rebellion against Moses, God's appointed leader. Korah challenged Moses' authority, contending that all the people of God were just as holy as their leader. To vindicate the authority of Moses and Aaron, God caused this rod to bud, blossom, and yield almonds overnight (Numbers 16 and 17).

The rod pictures the divine power of the Holy Spirit who brings life out of that which is dead, and it typifies the resurrection of Christ, the guarantee of our resurrection.

All three are needed. The three items that rested in the ark of the covenant represent three basic elements of the gospel we must fight to retain in the Church: divine truth or doctrine (the tablets); the supernatural working of God (the rod); and the reality of Christ (the manna).

Too often, little by little, denominations have lost these elements, until all that is left is correct doctrine—and sometimes mighty little of that. When all you have left is correct doctrine, then you have Pharisaism. Sad to say, some have even lost the element of truth, becoming "blind leaders of the blind." We need all three: divine truth, divine reality, and divine power.

God's Throne

The mercy seat was something special. In the outer court, one item was of brass, the other wood covered with brass. In the Holy Place, the golden candlestick was of solid gold, but the other two items were of wood covered with gold. The ark of the covenant was also part wood and part gold; but the mercy seat, a lid for the ark, was of solid gold.

Above the mercy seat, and part of it, were figures of two cherubim. It was the place where God, in a sense, dwelt in the midst of His people—it was His throne. Psalm 80:1 addresses God as the One who "dwellest between the cherubim."

The meaning of the mercy seat. What was the significance of this item of furniture? The words used in the original language to describe it show its purpose. The Hebrew word translated mercy seat means "covering." In the Septuagint Version, where a Greek synonym is used for this word, the meaning becomes even clearer—"propitiation."

The mercy seat covered the ark which contained the tablets of the Law. The original breaking of the tablets symbolized the countless times man has broken its laws. A cover was needed to shield the people from the condemnation for their sins. The mercy seat was this covering.

The justice of God. Love without justice is mushy sentimentality. You can see the beautiful mixture of love and justice in the Mercy Seat.

The cherubim, angelic representations of gold that were part of the mercy seat, symbolized the righteousness and justice of God. They looked down on the mercy seat that covered the ark.

A broken Law demands judgment, but God made a provision. Once a year on the Day of Atonement, the high priest would come with the blood of atonement and sprinkle it on the mercy seat. This meant that God, represented by the cherubim, saw not the broken Law, but the blood of atonement. God's grace covers all our sin.

Christ Is Our Mercy Seat

Romans 3:25 states that God has set Him forth "to be a propitiation." First John 2:2 also says that "he is the propitiation for our sins." In both places the word translated "propitiation" is the one used to describe *mercy seat*.

Jesus' righteousness covers all our sin, for He was without sin. He brings atonement through His own blood, not that of bulls and goats. Every man has sinned, but when the blood of Christ is applied our hearts become a mercy seat. There God the Father sees the blood of His Son; He considers our sins blotted out, and we are saved from judgment.

10
Our Great Representative

One section of the Congress of the United States in Washington, D. C. is called the House of Representatives. Every 2 years 435 men are elected to this body. While each state has two senators to represent it in the Senate, each member of the House represents a district in his state. While senators keep the interests of their entire state in mind, a member of the House of Representatives is answerable to a certain number of people and must take care of their interests.

In the high priest, the people of Israel had a man who represented them in a more important way than any elected government official. A more descriptive title would be mediator—someone who represented the people before God, and also represented God before the people.

The work of the high priest explains why the tabernacle was erected, the reason for the various sections of the building, and the purpose behind the various sacrifices. The preparation and ministry of the high priest, and especially what he did on the national Day of Atonement—all present some beautiful pictures of truth.

A Very Special Person

Without a doubt, according to the Book of Hebrews, the high priest of Israel was a type of Christ. Here are some passages that show this:

"We have a great high priest, that is passed into the heavens, Jesus the Son of God" (4:14). And verse 15 adds that He is One who can "be touched with the feeling of our infirmities."

Hebrews 7:24 says that He "hath an unchangeable priesthood." And verse 26 continues: "Such a high priest became us, who is holy, harmless, undefiled, separate from sinners, and made higher than the heavens." Then 8:1 proclaims: "We have such a high priest, who is set on the right hand of the throne of the Majesty in the heavens."

It seems that every detail of the high priest's life and ministry was a prophecy in type of what Jesus is and does. Since all believers are called to be priests unto God, it looks as though there must be many practical lessons in all this for us too.

Very Special Clothing

Because the high priest was to be a very special person, everything about his preparation for ministry was also very special, even the clothes he wore. Watch for the types of Christ and the practical lessons for us, as we proceed.

Before the high priest could put on his new clothing, he had to remove his old garments and take a complete bath. This was not the same as the daily washing of the hands and feet at the brazen laver before going to minister in the Holy Place.

What does this mean to us? When we come to Jesus for cleansing, we must put aside the clothes of the old life, the way we used to live. Then comes the cleansing by the blood of Christ, making us as clean as though we had never sinned. But we must go on from there. Each day we must make sure our lives are cleansed of any defilement that may have occurred.

A coat of fine linen. This was the first of the special garments for the high priest. It was worn next to the body. As I've pointed out before, the fine linen pictures the righteousness and purity of our Lord. We need it too.

The robe of the ephod. This was made of blue linen and was worn over the coat. The skirt of this robe had an interesting feature: alternating all along the hem of the robe were embroidered figures of pomegranates and little bells that tinkled as the high priest walked.

What a picture of Jesus, our heavenly High Priest! Blue, the heavenly color, speaks of the heavenly nature of Christ, and that His followers should be heavenly-minded people.

The pomegranates and the bells? They were symbols of fruitfulness and of testimony and praise. If we are to be priests who are like Jesus, we must have the fruit of the Spirit and a ringing testimony.

A well-balanced Christian life—that's what the equal number of pomegranates and bells speaks of. Our lives should contain a balance of fruitfulness and praise. Jesus' life did. How He acted matched what He said.

The ephod. "Someone is bearing your burdens," is what the ephod said. It was a short garment of linen with two shoulder pieces. On them were two onyx stones engraved with the names of the tribes of Israel, six names on each stone.

Exodus 28:12 explains the purpose of the stones: "Aaron shall bear their names before the Lord upon his two shoulders for a memorial." A beautiful type of how Christ, our great High Priest, carries our burdens before God's throne.

The breastplate. Made of the same fine linen as the ephod, the breastplate contained 12 different precious stones, each with the name of a tribe on it. "And Aaron shall bear the names of the children of Israel in the breastplate . . . for a memorial before the Lord continually" (v. 29).

Notice what this means. The names of God's people were carried before the Lord on the shoulders and over the heart of the high priest. Our High Priest's strength and love—they're ours!

The literal translation of 1 Peter 5:7 is: "Casting all your care upon him; for he has you on his heart." Doesn't that help you?

The mitre. This was a turbanlike hat. Across its front was a gold plate with the words *Holiness to the Lord* engraved on it. The head always symbolizes the mind, and it's here we need special protection. Temptation comes through the mind. If "holiness to the Lord" governs our thought life, then Satan can't get a foothold.

A Special Consecration

Before the high priest could begin his ministry as a representative for Israel before God, he had to go through a special ceremony after he had been bathed and the special clothing had been put on him.

The anointing oil. This was made from a unique formula. God had provided the information about the ingredients. The Israelites were forbidden to make any like it for their own use, and death was the penalty for duplicating it (see Exodus 30:31,33).

You've probably guessed the meaning of the oil—the Holy Spirit. A person may have been cleansed from his sins at Calvary. That's fine. But before he can minister effectively for the Lord, he needs the special anointing of the Holy Spirit.

Jesus had such an anointing. In fact, the Hebrew word translated "Messiah," and the Greek word translated "Christ," both have the same basic meaning: "The Anointed One." Three types of leaders were anointed in Old Testament times—kings, priests, and prophets. They pointed forward to the One who was to come; the One who was specially anointed to be Prophet, Priest, and King.

The sacrifice. Three animals were offered when a high priest was consecrated to his ministry: a bullock for a sin offering; a ram for a burnt offering, which was completely burned; and another ram of consecration, part of which was eaten by the priests.

The bullock typified Christ, our great Sin Offering, who died for us on Calvary. Aaron and his sons, by laying their hands on the bullock and confessing their sins, transferred their sins, by faith, to the animal. Next they killed it, poured the blood out at the brazen altar, and burned the rest of the bullock on the altar.

Do you see the similarity? By faith we may transfer our sins to Jesus. We believe His blood was poured out for our salvation and He suffered our punishment.

Then the two rams were brought. The first was killed, cut into pieces, washed, and entirely burned on the brazen altar as a burnt offering. The Hebrew word for "burnt offering" explains its meaning—"the whole thing—going up." Again it pictures Jesus' complete consecration in life and in death. "I come . . . to do thy will, O God" (Hebrews 10:7).

Though the second ram was also one of consecration, it had a very specific relationship to the priests. The blood of this animal was put on the right ear, thumb, and large toe of Aaron and his sons, and the breast and the shoulder were given to them to eat.

The blood on the ear represents a consecrated will. We should listen to the voice of God, rather than the voice of the world. The blood on the thumb represents consecrated service. All our talents and abilities should be consecrated to the work of God. And the blood on the large toe represents consecrated living. Listening to God and working for Him are important, but our daily walk should be pleasing to Him.

A Very Special Ministry

The high priest of Israel constantly served the people as their mediator before God. But his work on the Day of Atonement was the most significant of the entire year.

This was the day of all days for the Israelites. Once a year an atoning sacrifice was offered for the sins of the entire nation. It was then the Old Testament provision for pardon reached its climax. It pictured the atoning work of Christ, done once for all.

Atonement for the high priest. The high priest had to perform every duty this day with great care.

1. He offered a bullock as a sin offering for himself and his family.

2. He carried the animal's blood in a basin into the Holy Place.

3. He took from the golden altar of incense some live coals and placed them with incense in a censer.

4. Only then did he dare to pull aside the veil into the Holy of Holies. The billowing smoke from the incense hid the mercy seat from view. If the priest failed to do this, he would die. (See Leviticus 16:13.)

5. With his finger the high priest sprinkled the blood on the mercy seat and in front of it seven times. Only

with the blood of atonement did he dare come into the Holy of Holies.

A Very Special Offering

After making atonement for himself, the high priest returned to the door of the tabernacle, where two goats were brought before him. By casting lots, one goat (called the Lord's goat) was chosen to be sacrificed on the brazen altar. The other goat was called the goat for the people or the "scapegoat."

The goats represented two parts of one offering. One pictured the means by which atonement was made, the other, the results of atonement.

Atonement. The high priest killed the Lord's goat and offered it on the brazen altar. Then taking some of the blood, he entered once more into the Holy of Holies and sprinkled the blood seven times. He also put part of that blood and the blood of the offering he had made for himself on the altar of incense. Finally, the body of the bullock that had been offered as a sin offering was burned outside the camp.

What a beautiful picture of the atonement Jesus wrought for us! On Calvary Jesus became our Sin Offering. His blood was presented in the presence of God at the heavenly mercy seat and accepted there for us. The blood on the altar of incense (which signifies prayer) means that we now have access into the presence of God. As the animal was burned outside the camp, Jesus died on Calvary, which was outside the city of Jerusalem. Hebrews 13:11, 12 explains this.

A Special Ceremony

The goat for the people was called the "scapegoat." At the door of the tabernacle the high priest laid his hands on it, confessing the sins of the people. Then the scapegoat was sent away into the wilderness, never to return again.

We can rejoice in the meaning of the scapegoat! Jesus died for our sins and cleansed us by His blood. But more than that, He sends them away, never to be remembered against us anymore. As the Israelite watched the scapegoat disappear, he could shout, "There go my sins!" We can say that too!

It was an awesome time when the high priest entered the Holy of Holies. The people stood breathlessly, fearing he might die if he disobeyed any of God's commands. How they rejoiced as they heard the tinkling of the bells on the skirts of his garment. They knew he was alive. God had accepted the sacrifice.

After Jesus died on the cross, He ascended to the presence of God and presented blood, not that of an animal but His own. On earth, in the Upper Room, His followers listened for a sign that the Sacrifice had been accepted. They heard a sound from heaven! The coming of the Holy Spirit on the Day of Pentecost brought indisputable proof that the Atonement was complete.

11
The Way Through the Wilderness

Paul begins chapter 10 of 1 Corinthians by warning fellow believers that the Children of Israel in Moses' day displeased God with their sinful practices. If Paul were using modern speech, he might warn the Corinthians in this manner: "These things are examples to us lest we long for the things of the world, lest we go back to sin, in our hearts first and then in our actions. Neither let us be idolaters by putting our homes, our children, our jobs, or our friends ahead of God. Neither let us doubt the goodness of God when trials come. But Jesus will help us, for He is our way of escape."

Some people don't like the Old Testament and perhaps wonder why we have been spending so much time on the tabernacle. But in 1 Corinthians 10:11 Paul clearly shows that the events of Israel's history have great meaning for us.

Pay attention to what he is saying: "Now all these things happened unto them for ensamples: and they are written for our admonition, upon whom the ends of the world are come."

As we learned in chapter 1, the word *ensamples* (examples) can be translated "types," and that's what this study is all about.

As we watch Israel leaving Egypt and traveling toward the Promised Land, we can see a symbolic picture of the Christian life. The various places they camped; the events that happened to them; their failures and victories—we find the counterparts in our Christian experience.

Salvation

Egypt, of course, is a type of sin. Just as Israel's real life as a nation began when she left the land of her bondage, so we really begin to live when we stop living in sin.

Notice the parallels: Israel, in Egypt, was in bitter bondage. She was in danger of extinction, with every male baby born under the sentence of death. For us sin means bondage also. Think of the pitiful victims of liquor and tobacco habits. Sin also means death—eternal death.

How did Israel escape from Egypt? By supernatural demonstrations of God's power: the plagues, the sword of the angel of death, and the miraculous parting of the Red Sea.

How did you get free from sin? It had to be by a miracle. As John Peterson says in his lovely song, "It took a miracle of love and grace."

Salvation isn't just joining a church, turning over a new leaf, or making some good resolutions. Not joining a church, but joining Jesus. Not turning over a new leaf, but getting a new life. Not making good resolutions but having a heart revolution.

Liberals try to explain away the Red Sea miracle. "It's simple to understand," such a preacher proclaimed. "At the place where the Israelites crossed, it happened that the water was only about 2 feet deep."

"Praise the Lord!" shouted a simple believer.

"Why are you praising the Lord over that?" demanded the preacher.

"For the miracle."

"The miracle?"

"Yes, if the water was only 2 feet deep, it took a miracle for all the Egyptians and their horses to get drowned!"

According to Paul, the Israelites were "baptized unto Moses in the cloud and in the sea" (1 Corinthians 10:2). That is, they became his followers.

Our baptism in water proclaims our separation from the old life and our decision to follow Jesus.

Blessing After Bitterness

"We are on our way to Canaan, shouting, 'Glory,' " the Israelites might well have sung. But they found out, as most new converts do, that the Christian life is not always an easy one. They ran out of water, and when they found some it was so bitter that they called the place "Marah," meaning "bitterness."

What were they to do for the throng of about 3 million people? God showed Moses a tree which he threw into the water, and it became sweet. Then the Lord led them to Elim, a lovely oasis with 12 wells (or springs) and 70 palm trees.

A new convert who thinks he will have no problems already has a problem. He hasn't reached heaven yet. And there are some bitter places.

You may wonder why you have some of the same trials as sinners. "Isn't there supposed to be a difference when you live for the Lord?" you might say.

Oh, there is! The tree at Marah represents the cross of Christ. Calvary brings sweetness to the bitter places of life. And we have our Elims too—places of refreshment, peace, and rest.

Divine Revelation

A Jewish taxi driver in Philadelphia blamed Moses for Israel's present problems: "He should have made a right turn to Saudi Arabia, where the oil is, instead of a left turn to Palestine!"

But God had made an appointment with Moses. Before turning north toward Canaan, they *did* turn south briefly to reach Mt. Sinai.

Sinai was a landmark event in Israel's history. There they had a revelation of God (especially Moses). There they received the tables of the Law written with the very finger of God. The Feast of Pentecost (meaning "50 days after") is believed to commemorate the giving of the Law 50 days after they left Egypt.

You've left the Egypt of sin? Great! But that's not enough. God wants to reveal himself to you in an even greater way. You can have a personal "Day of Pentecost." What happened in the Upper Room after Jesus' ascension can happen to you. If they needed a supernatural outpouring so they could minister for God in the power of the Holy Spirit, don't you think *you* do? How about visiting Mt. Sinai?

A Place of Decision

Kadesh-barnea was a dark chapter in Israel's history. There, at the border of the Promised Land, at the insistence of the tribal leaders, Moses sent 12 men to spy out the land.

Now, it's okay to plan ahead, but that was not the case with these men. God had already told them they were to have the land, so their concern should have been to find out how they would conquer it. Instead, they went to check out whether or not they should *try* to conquer it. Quite a difference!

What a land it was! They came back with glowing reports. But 10 of them also came back with exaggerated accounts of the difficulties. Giants so big they made the Israelites feel like grasshoppers. Cities walled up to heaven—obviously untrue. But the people believed them. Disillusioned, they turned their backs on God's promises. For 38 more years (a total of 40) they wandered, until the bones of all the adults bleached in the desert sun.

The most important lesson of all: at the end of that time, they came back to Kadesh-barnea again. If God brings us to a place of decision and we fail to do His will, we shall never go any farther until we have met and conquered that problem.

Dangers for God's People

As Paul points out in 1 Corinthians 10, Israel's failures in the wilderness have a spiritual application for us. We can fail in the same way they did.

Wrong desires. According to Numbers 11:4, 5, the "mixed multitude that was among them fell a lusting" after the food they had formerly enjoyed in Egypt. Their steady diet of manna was just too much for them, it seems. Let us also be careful lest we look back toward the world (which Egypt typifies) and are tempted to go back or to doubt God's goodness.

Spiritual idolatry. Of course, you're not going to be tempted to make a golden calf and worship it as Israel did. But for us an idol is anything that takes the chief place in our lives that belongs only to God.

Unfaithfulness. Israelite men entered into immoral relations with the women of Midian (Numbers 25) just before the nation crossed Jordan. Many died in the plague God sent. Our relationship to Christ is like that of a girl engaged to be married. Let us be true to Him.

Rebellion. At one time, the Israelites "spake against God, and against Moses" (Numbers 21:5). The result was a plague of serpents among them. Sometimes it's difficult to understand all God is trying to do with our lives, but that's the time to trust the Lord. Complaining often results in rebellion against His leadership. In spite of trials that come our way, Christians "never had it so good."

Murmuring. We may think of Israel, "What a bunch of soreheads!" Over and over they griped about this or that. As a result, many died in the wilderness and never reached Canaan. When we murmur today, we are actually saying God is not good, not faithful—and you know that isn't true.

Everything Needed

It's good some of us are not God. We would never have put up with all the doubting and murmuring. But God's not like us. Every mile of the way God was with His people, watching over them. He may not have satisfied all their wants, but He supplied all their needs. And in so doing He pictured what He will do for His people in these days.

A Sign and a Signal

Billowing up from the part of the tabernacle that contained the Holy of Holies was the cloud called the "Shekinah" (the "Presence"). During the day it spread out over the entire encampment, shielding them from the blazing rays of the sun. At night the pillar of fire provided light for the camp.

We too have the "Presence" of God with us in the form of the Holy Spirit. What the pillar of fire by night and the cloud by day meant to Israel, the Spirit of God means to us. God lives in us by the Spirit.

When the cloud moved, Israel knew they were to move also. It was a signal for them. The cloud went before them as a guide. The Holy Spirit is our means of guidance today. Because He knows what God's will is for us, He will help us find that will. He will lead us to God and our eternal home.

Food for the Hungry

Where were the Israelites to find enough food for that great throng? God solved their dietary problem by providing food in a supernatural way. Each morning when the dew had vanished, there was food on the ground. "Manna!" the people cried, meaning, "What is it?" And so that's what they called the strange food. It may not have tasted like filet mignon, but it was sufficient for their needs.

The manna typifies Christ. He said: "I am that bread of life" (John 6:48). By having fellowship with Him in prayer and reading the Word, we receive spiritual nourishment. We receive of His life.

Remember this: the people had to gather a fresh supply each morning. They couldn't keep it over night. Do you ever think your experience seems stale? Perhaps there's a good reason.

Have a Cool Drink

One of the greatest demonstrations of God's power occurred at Rephidim. When the people complained because there was no water, Moses took the matter to God. Then at God's command he took the rod and struck a huge rock—and a river of water gushed out.

What does this signify? First Corinthians 10:4 states: "They drank of that spiritual Rock that followed them; and that Rock was Christ." The rock Moses struck is a beautiful picture of Christ, smitten so streams of blessing can flow.

Each year at the Feast of Tabernacles Israel celebrated this event. At one such feast Jesus stood and declared: "If any man thirst, let him come unto me, and drink" (John 7:37). So it's clear the rock was a type of Christ.

The water represents the Holy Spirit. Jesus spoke of the "rivers of living water," which would flow out of the believer, as meaning the Holy Spirit (John 7:38, 39). Let the rivers flow!

12
The Only Way to God

In the year 1628 an English scientist, William Harvey, announced one of the greatest discoveries of all time—the true nature of the circulation of the blood.

The Book of Knowledge encyclopedia says concerning this: "All real knowledge of the working of the body dates from that time. This is one of those great discoveries that opens the door to whole realms of nature."

Before the time of Harvey's studies, men did not understand how the blood is pumped by the heart through the whole body, making a complete circuit and coming back again. Now physicians know that without the blood there is no life. The blood carries nourishment to all parts of the body. It fights disease. It brings life. As the Bible declares, we are "fearfully and wonderfully made" (Psalm 139:14).

William Harvey deserves our praise, but actually he only discovered what the Lord said to Moses long ago: "The life of the flesh is in the blood" (Leviticus 17:11). The Bible is always ahead of its time.

But there's an even greater discovery men may make about the blood—greater than the findings of William Harvey. In Leviticus 17:11 God said something more about the blood: "I have given it to you upon the altar to make an atonement for your souls: for it is the blood that maketh an atonement for the soul."

What was God saying? That while our natural blood brings healing and health to our natural bodies, He has provided a means, by blood, whereby we may have not merely natural life but eternal life.

God's Great Purpose

Why did God provide Moses with the design for the tabernacle? Why did He establish the priesthood? Why did He give all the laws of the Mosaic code? The whole system was to provide a means by which sinful man might approach a holy God. The building of the tabernacle and the installation of the priests was all preliminary to what God wanted to do.

He wanted men to be able to come to Him. Since He is the very essence of holiness and men are basically sinful, something had to be done about sin. So God provided a means of atonement through the system of blood sacrifices.

Let's quickly review the principle behind the Old Testament offerings, which God himself established. As a sinner, man is doomed, but God has planned to save him. God's law provides death for sin, but God has provided a way of escape. All who were ever born on this earth have sinned—except One, Jesus Christ. Because He never sinned, God accepts Jesus' life in place of the sinner's life.

God's Visual Aid Board

Sunday school teachers often place figures on a flannelboard to illustrate truths they are trying to teach. Think of the Book of Leviticus as a gigantic visual-aid board on which God has spread out vivid pictures of Redemption.

Paul refers to the deeper teachings of the Word of God as "strong meat." But let us allow the Holy Spirit to take us on a guided tour to inspect the meaning of these offerings. If we follow His leadership, He will take us into the Holy of Holies of scriptural truth.

The Importance of the Blood

We must think of the blood of the Old Testament sacrifices as typical of the blood of Jesus Christ. Even the typical blood filled an important role. But if the blood of animals could make atonement for sin, how much more is this true of the blood of Christ!

The Bible makes a fine distinction between what the blood of the animal sacrifices and the blood of Jesus can do. The Old Testament Hebrew word for "atonement" is *kaphar*. It means "to cover." The blood acted like a screen, hiding the sin from God's eyes, so He would not send judgment on the soul that had been covered by the blood. This was effective for the Old Testament era, but God had something better than that.

Though the blood of the Old Testament animal sacrifices covered sin, it couldn't take sin away. "For it is not possible that the blood of bulls and of goats should take away sins" (Hebrews 10:4).

Perhaps you're asking: "Why wasn't one kind of blood as good as another?"

Here's why: (1) An animal is incapable of independent thought and moral feeling, so it could not be a perfect substitute for man. (2) Although the animal was the means by which atonement came, it was not a personal, voluntary act by the animal.

So what was the value of the animal sacrifices? They pointed forward to the coming of a perfect Sacrifice, One who had been foreordained to such a work before the worlds came into existence. The offerings typified the coming of Christ who would give himself for the sins of all mankind.

In Old Testament times, one animal for one man was the method. When Jesus came, one Offering became sufficient for all mankind, past, present, and future.

Now, let's look at three offerings that have a tremendous application to the Christian experience. Notice the similarities and the contrasts.

An Offering for Cleansing
[*The Sin Offering*]

An offering for sin was something new. Nations prior to the time of Moses had used the other offerings. So had the patriarchs. But now by establishing the Law, God was emphasizing sin and guilt in a new way. It spoke of atonement, cleansing for sin, through the shedding of blood.

Here's how the sacrifice was made. A man who had sinned brought his sin offering to the brazen altar in the outer court of the tabernacle, and the animal was laid on the altar. Then the man laid his hands on the animal that was to be sacrificed. By doing this he was admitting himself to be a sinner, and by faith was transferring his guilt to the sacrifice. The priest then killed the animal, a substitute for the man. Some of the blood was sprinkled on the horns of the brazen altar, while the rest was poured out at the bottom of the altar.

Sounds rather gory, doesn't it? But wait! If you grasp the spiritual significance of all this, you will thrill to the beautiful picture of atonement that it presents.

A Drama of Redemption

Think of it! Jesus was our Sin Offering. Not a dumb, unreasoning animal without any of the finer sensibilities, selected only for its physical acceptability. Our Sacrifice was Jesus Christ, the Son of God. He was without sin, but He was willing to take our sin upon himself.

Here is a very significant fact: the sin offering and the sinner were so closely connected in God's view of things, He looked on both as one. So when Jesus became our Sin Offering, He identified himself with our sins. No wonder the Father could not bear to look on Him as He hung on the cross.

There's a great contrast between the animal sacrifice and the offering of God's Lamb. The animal had no "say" in what was done. But no one took Jesus' life from Him. He "gave himself for our sins" (Galatians 1:4). This was why He came into the world. He has "appeared to put away sin by the sacrifice of himself" (Hebrews 9:26).

We have a part to play in this drama. Like the Israelite of old, we must admit our need of forgiveness. We must take Jesus as our Substitute.

Related to the sin offering, the trespass offering dealt with specific acts of sin. The sin offering, then, pictures the atonement for man's sinful nature; the trespass offering, atonement for the specific acts. Jesus died not only for our *sin* but also for our *sins*.

An Offering for Consecration
[*The Burnt Offering*]

When a person sacrificed a burnt offering, he was acknowledging that complete consecration to God is a necessary ingredient in genuine worship.

The Hebrew words used to describe the burnt offering conveyed the idea of a sacrifice that was completely burned. This was the feature that made it different from the other offerings.

Atonement. The burnt offering also conveyed the idea of atonement. Atoning blood must be shed.

What a lesson this teaches. Consecration, no matter how great, is insufficient to obtain God's favor unless, first, atonement has been made.

The ascending smoke. As the smoke rose, it represented the man's desire to give himself to God as completely as the sacrifice being consumed on the altar. Because he was unable to, the blood atoned for him.

A Perfect Sacrifice

The animal had to be without blemish. After it had been killed, it was cut in pieces and burned on the brazen altar.

Jesus was our Burnt Offering. "Through the eternal Spirit [He] offered himself without spot to God" (Hebrews 9:14). This takes us to Gethsemane to watch Jesus as He shrinks from taking our sins upon himself; but He says: "Nevertheless, not my will, but thine, be done" (Luke 22:42).

The other offerings were for special occasions, but the burnt offering was on a regular schedule. God commanded that it be offered every morning and every evening (Leviticus 6:8-12). For this reason the priests were to keep the fire ever burning on the brazen altar. "The fire shall ever be burning upon the altar; it shall never go out" (v. 13).

What a lesson this conveys to us. We are so constituted that one act of consecration is not enough; it must be constantly renewed. If we will keep the fires of dedication always burning on the altars of our hearts, then day by day we can constantly consecrate all of our lives to Him.

Notice it was the Israelite himself, not a priest, who killed the animal. When we make a consecration to the Lord we should be personally involved in it. No one can make the consecration for us. We must face the issue ourselves, fully aware of what it will cost us. It must be voluntary, then it will be effective.

Here's something interesting. The Hebrew word used to describe the burning of the burnt offering is a different word from that used to describe the burning of the sin offering. The word used with the sin offering refers to bearing the wrath of God, but the word used with the burnt offering carries the idea of sending heavenward a "sweet savor" (pleasing odor) unto the Lord. Consecration to God is like a beautiful perfume and fragrance to God.

An Offering for Communion
[*The Peace Offering*]

The peace offering was offered at feasts, for it was a sacrifice that ended in a meal. It expressed peace and fellowship with God resulting from the blood atonement. It was the most joyous of the sacrifices.

It was a time of sharing. God's portion of the sacrifice was burned on the altar; part was given to the priests as their appointed portion; and part was for the worshiper himself to feast on. It was a time of fellowship with God!

An Israelite offered a peace offering to God on one of three occasions: (1) to express thanksgiving to God for blessings he had received; (2) to fulfill a vow he had made if he received certain benefits; or (3) to present a freewill offering as a spontaneous expression of love to God and a desire to be in fellowship with Him. Even with such an offering, the idea of atonement was present.

What does the peace offering mean to us? A means of reaching God. Sin has always stood in the way, but Jesus is our Peace Offering. The Father always accepts Him, and when we are in Him through salvation we become "accepted in the beloved" (Ephesians 1:6).

Remember, God has always wanted fellowship with man. By becoming the Offering for sin, Jesus became the great bridge of reconciliation. Over it man can reach God, and God can reach man. "God . . . hath reconciled us to himself by Jesus Christ" (2 Corinthians 5:18).

To the Israelite, eating part of the sacrifice symbolized peace and fellowship with God. What a privilege we also have to come into a living relationship with God the Father and His Son Jesus Christ.

13
Happy Holidays

Americans will never forget the great Bicentennial celebration, especially the climax on July 4, 1976. From the Atlantic to the Pacific, the nation rejoiced in the 200th anniversary of its birth. It was one of the happiest days in the history of the United States.

Israel also had special holidays to celebrate outstanding events in her history. And as the great Hebrew scholar Myer Pearlman observed, the early histories of Israel and the United States are similar.

There were 13 tribes who wanted to be set free from what they considered an unjust rule. They were led by a great leader who put his trust in God. They went through great privations while conquering a wilderness.

Interestingly, the three great feasts of Israel commemorated events strikingly similar to those in the history of America. Two of these, Independence Day and Thanksgiving Day, Americans celebrate with a 1-day holiday. For Israel 1 day wasn't enough. For each of their holidays they took 7 days!

Independence Day. At the Feast of Passover, the Israelites could look back and thank God for their deliverance from captivity and death. They had been set free from Egypt's rule.

"Constitutional Convention." Americans remember the great sessions that gave their country a constitution, by which the founding fathers charted the course of the nation. The Feast of Pentecost celebrated the giving of the Law at Mt. Sinai, when God gave them their "constitution and bylaws."

Thanksgiving Days. For 7 days each year Israel remembered with thankfulness how God had helped their ancestors during their wilderness wanderings.

Israel's happy holidays had a spiritual meaning to them—and even more to us. Paul points out that Christ is our Passover, bringing freedom from sin. He is the "greater than Moses" who gives something better than the Law—the Spirit of God. He brings the Feast of Tabernacles into present-tense focus, for He is Immanuel, "God with us"; God tabernacling, living among His people.

A Glorious Past

Each of Israel's feasts commemorated a great event of the past.

The Feast of Passover celebrated the time when the last of 10 plagues forced Pharaoh to give up and let the Israelites leave the land of Egypt. When the firstborn in every Egyptian home died, including Pharaoh's own son, the king could stand against God no longer. However, the firstborn sons of the Israelites were spared because a lamb had been slain and the blood sprinkled on the two sideposts and over the door.

The Feast of Pentecost reminded Israel of the time when they arrived at Mount Sinai and received the Law, as God revealed himself to them. Talk about fireworks! God put on a display that even America's Bicentennial could not equal. "Mount Sinai was altogether on a smoke, because the Lord descended upon it in fire: and the smoke thereof ascended as the smoke of a furnace, and the whole mount quaked greatly'' (Exodus 19:18).

The Feast of Tabernacles commemorated the years of wandering in the wilderness. The children especially must have loved it. The Israelites made booths (shelters) of branches from various trees and camped outside for 7 days.

Good Times in the Present

Israel's happy holidays were related to their times of harvest. At Passover time they offered to the Lord a sheaf of grain, the firstfruits of their harvest. Pentecost was also called the "Feast of Weeks" because it was celebrated 7 weeks after Passover. They had begun to put the sickle to the corn, so they offered two wave loaves before the Lord. The Feast of Tabernacles, a time of general thanksgiving, was observed 7 days after the end of harvest.

Hope for the Future

Now comes the meaning for us. All that happened to Israel in Old Testament times has a significance for us.

The Feast of Passover pointed forward to Calvary. Like the lamb slain in Egypt to save the firstborn, Jesus, the Lamb of God, died to save the world.

Pentecost foretold the descent of the Holy Spirit on the Day of Pentecost (Acts 2). The Spirit came 50 days after Jesus' death. That's the reason the disciples had to tarry—until the Day of Pentecost was *fully* come—to fulfill the type perfectly.

Good news! Today believers don't have to wait even 10 minutes, let alone 10 days.

The Feast of Tabernacles is the only one yet to be fulfilled. It points forward to the gathering of all kindreds, nations, and people to the great harvest in heaven.

Celebrating Independence Day

Each Passover, all Israel looked back to the time when God delivered them from Egypt.

God's lamb. Exodus 12:3-5, 11-13 records God's explicit rules concerning the animal used for sacrifice. It was to be a lamb in its prime, "a male of the first year." It was to be without blemish, set apart 4 days before the day of Passover. It was slain, roasted, and eaten. The entire congregation had to take part. Interestingly, not a bone was to be broken.

Jesus fulfills the type. Jesus offered himself as a sacrifice for sin, not as an infant but at the height of His mature strength. Jesus was pure, without blemish (1 Peter 1:19). Even Pilate, who sentenced Him, said he found no fault in Him. He was completely innocent.

Jesus was also set apart. God the Father had planned Redemption before the creation of the universe, and the Son had been designated for this work. It's interesting to note that Jesus entered Jerusalem 4 days before the Passover.

The fires that cooked the Passover lamb vividly picture the tremendous suffering Jesus endured in bearing our sins, sorrows, and sicknesses on the cross. He was "made a curse for us" (Galatians 3:13). He suffered the penalty of hell.

All Israel took part in Jesus' condemnation. When Pilate gave the rulers a choice between Jesus and Barabbas, "They cried out all at once, saying, Away with this man, and release unto us Barabbas" (Luke 23:18).

As in the case of the Passover lamb, not one bone of our Lord was broken. When the soldiers came to break

His legs to hasten death (as the custom was), they found it unnecessary, for Jesus was already dead (John 19:33,36).

The precious Blood. It was not enough for the blood of the lamb to be shed, it had to be applied to the doorposts and the lintel. A small bit of hyssop was used to do this. Thus applied, it became the means of preservation, for the firstborn in those homes were spared when the Lord passed over.

What a picture of what Jesus' blood means to us! It was shed on Calvary, but it must be applied to our hearts. By faith we use the promises in the Word to do this. Its being placed on the doorposts represents an open confession. That it was not placed on the threshold means we must reverence it; it is precious (Hebrews 10:29; 1 Peter 1:19). And it brings protection from the wrath of God, the curse of the Law, and the damnation of hell (Romans 8:1).

Make the Lamb a part of your life. God did not intend the Passover lamb to be merely looked at but to be eaten. It was to be done immediately (Exodus 12:10), and the Israelites were to be ready to leave (v. 11).

We must not just know about Jesus or even admire Him. This is not enough. We must appropriate Him; take Him into our lives. And we must not wait. "Now is the day of salvation" (2 Corinthians 6:2). Finally, we must be ready to leave the world behind, saying good-bye to sin and Satan.

Remembering the "Constitutional Convention"

The delegates to the meeting in Philadelphia that were to draw up a constitution for the new nation following the Revolutionary War, met for long, weary months. It seemed they had reached a stalemate. Then the venerable Benjamin Franklin arose and spoke to them.

The God who had guided the destiny of the infant nation had shown himself so concerned about His creation that He noticed when even a sparrow fell. Would He not respond then if the delegates would ask Him for guidance? When they did so, the atmosphere of the meeting changed dramatically, and with ease they completed one of the great documents of history.

Accepting God's Government

Fifty days after (this is what "Pentecost" means) Israel was delivered from Egypt, the marching multitude reached Mount Sinai. They were a motley group, disorganized and unused to ruling themselves. They needed help.

God himself was "Chairman" of their "constitutional convention." He provided the laws by which they would be governed and spelled out the details—even to matters of diet and personal cleanliness.

At Pentecost the infant Church learned how they would be governed—by the rule of the Spirit. As Moses was to Israel, the Holy Spirit became the Leader of the Church. Indeed, this is one of the great signs that we belong to the family of God, the Church. "For as many as are led by the Spirit of God, they are the sons of God" (Romans 8:14).

A New Kind of Law

The laws of God's new kingdom are not like the law of Moses, written out in minute detail. Instead, the Holy Spirit who lives within believers guides us into all truth.

The Ten Commandments written on the two tables of stone have long since vanished. We have something better. Paul states it: "Written not with ink, but with the Spirit of the living God; not in tables of stone, but in fleshly tables of the heart" (2 Corinthians 3:3).

Celebrating a Harvest

There was a close relationship between the Feasts of Passover and Pentecost. The sheaf of firstfruits, at the beginning of the harvest, was presented at Passover time. At Pentecost, two loaves made from the wheat of the completed harvest were presented to the Lord.

Jesus was crucified at Passover time—the corn of wheat that had to die to produce a harvest (John 12:24). But the sheaf of firstfruits speaks of the Resurrection: Jesus, "the firstfruits of them that slept" (1 Corinthians 15:20).

Then on the Day of Pentecost, the first of a great harvest, 3000 souls, was gathered; the beginning of the great ingathering of the centuries to come.

Two loaves were offered. Is this not typical of the harvest from both Jews and Gentiles?

Celebrating Thanksgiving Day

The Feast of Tabernacles, or *Ingathering,* was a time of great joy. It reminded the Israelites of how God had been with His people in the wilderness. But it also celebrated the final gathering of their harvests. Even today in the reborn nation of Israel, many live outdoors during this time.

Two great ceremonies, though not described in the Bible, were connected with this observance during the days of Jesus' life on earth: (1) Each day of the feast water was brought from the Pool of Siloam and poured at the foot of the brazen altar, commemorating the miracle when God brought water from the rock at

Rephidim. (2) At night the temple area was lighted with great candlesticks, and there was great joy as the people remembered the pillar of fire in the wilderness.

It was with a background like this that Jesus said to these people who knew the form of religion but not the power: "If any man thirst, let him come unto me, and drink" (John 7:37). They had only the memory; Jesus had the living water. And in John 8 Jesus undoubtedly referred to the display of light when He proclaimed: "I am the light of the world: he that followeth me shall not walk in darkness, but shall have the light of life" (v. 12).

Thanksgiving Day is a joyous occasion. Families often get together. Christians remember the goodness of God. But the types of the past and the customs of today can provide only a dim outline of what lies ahead for the people of God. The harvest of souls will finally be complete. Think of the rejoicing on the other side when the redeemed from all ages and every tribe, tongue, and nation shall gather around the Throne. That will be the greatest Thanksgiving Day of all!

Glossary of Types

ACTIONS

Baptism—death, burial, resurrection
Eating—assimilation (as doctrine)
Offerings
   Burnt—consecration
   Meat—receiving strength from Christ
   Peace—communion with God
   Sin, trespass—Christ, our Sinbearer
Weeping—sorrow, humility
Walking—conduct
War—spiritual conflict
Washing—cleansing

CLOTHING

Ephod—Christ, our High Priest
Garment—covering of righteousness, evil
Girdle, belt—gathering strength
Linen—purity

COLORS

Blue—heaven, or heavenly things
Crimson—suffering, or sacrifice
Red—same as crimson
Scarlet—same as crimson
White—purity, righteousness

CREATURES

Birds—spirit beings, usually evil
Bullock, oxen—strength or service

Fish—men
Goat—sin, or the sinner
Lamb, ram—Christ, the Perfect Offering
Lion—rulership
Serpent—Satan
Sheep—God's people

FOOD

Bread—means of sustaining life
Fat—energy
Fruit—increase or multiplication
Honey—natural sweetness, man's best efforts
Leaven—sin, hypocrisy
Manna—Christ, the Bread of Life
Meat—strong spiritual food
Milk—spiritual food for young believers
Salt—incorruptibility, or faithfulness
Wine—teaching: fermented, false; unfermented, true

HUMAN BODY

Arm—strength and power
Ear—listening
Eye—knowledge
Feet—walk, or conduct
Fingers—work
Hair—strength
Hand—possession, strength, action
Head—thoughts, or lordship
Heart—the center, or love
Lips, mouth—testimony
Shoulder—strength for burdens

METALS

Brass—judgment, or endurance
Gold—glory, or supremacy
Silver—redemption

NATURAL PHENOMENA

Fire—presence of God in favor or judgment
Flood—judgment
Rain—blessing
Snow—purity
Wind—might, power

OBJECTS

Altar—sacrifice, or worship
Ark of covenant—Christ, our Mediator
Ark of Noah—safety in Christ
Crown—rulership
Door—entrance
Feathers—protection, or covering
Golden candlestick—testimony
Key—authority, or knowledge
Mercy seat—Christ, our Propitiation
Rod—rulership, or guidance
Sword—the Word of God
Veil—the flesh of Christ
Wood—humanity

PEOPLE

Aaron—Christ, our High Priest
Abraham—God the Father
David—Christ as King
Esau—the sensual, natural man
Isaac—Christ, the obedient Son
Jacob—spiritual man, contrasted with Esau
Joseph—Christ, suffering and glorified
Joshua—Christ as our Leader
Leper—the sinner
Melchizedek—Christ, Priest and King
Moses—Christ, Deliverer and Ruler
Priest—Christ, our High Priest
Shepherd—Christ, the Good Shepherd

PLACES

Desert—temptation, or persecution
Egypt—sin, or the world
Canaan—Spirit-filled life, or heaven
Gomorrah, Sodom—wickedness
Jerusalem—the celestial city, or heaven
Refuge, cities of—Christ, our Protection
Rephidim—refreshing, or life of the Spirit
Wilderness—life of a carnal Christian

ARRANGEMENT OF THE TABERNACLE FURNITURE

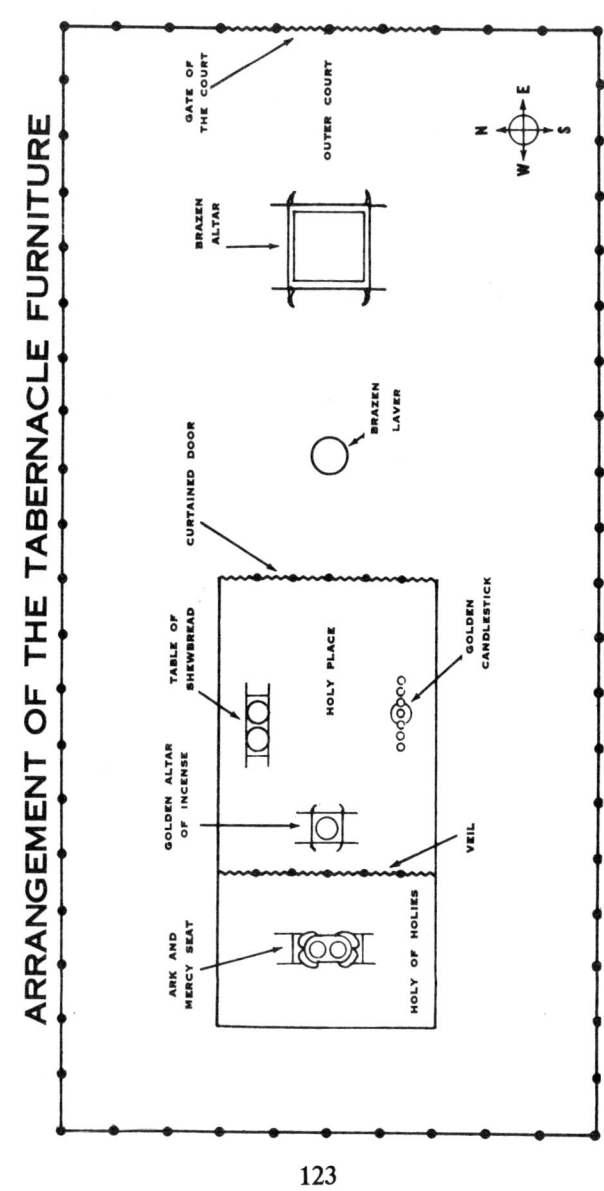